Mental Mathematics Practice 1

• Algebra • Shape • Data Handling
• Number • Measurement

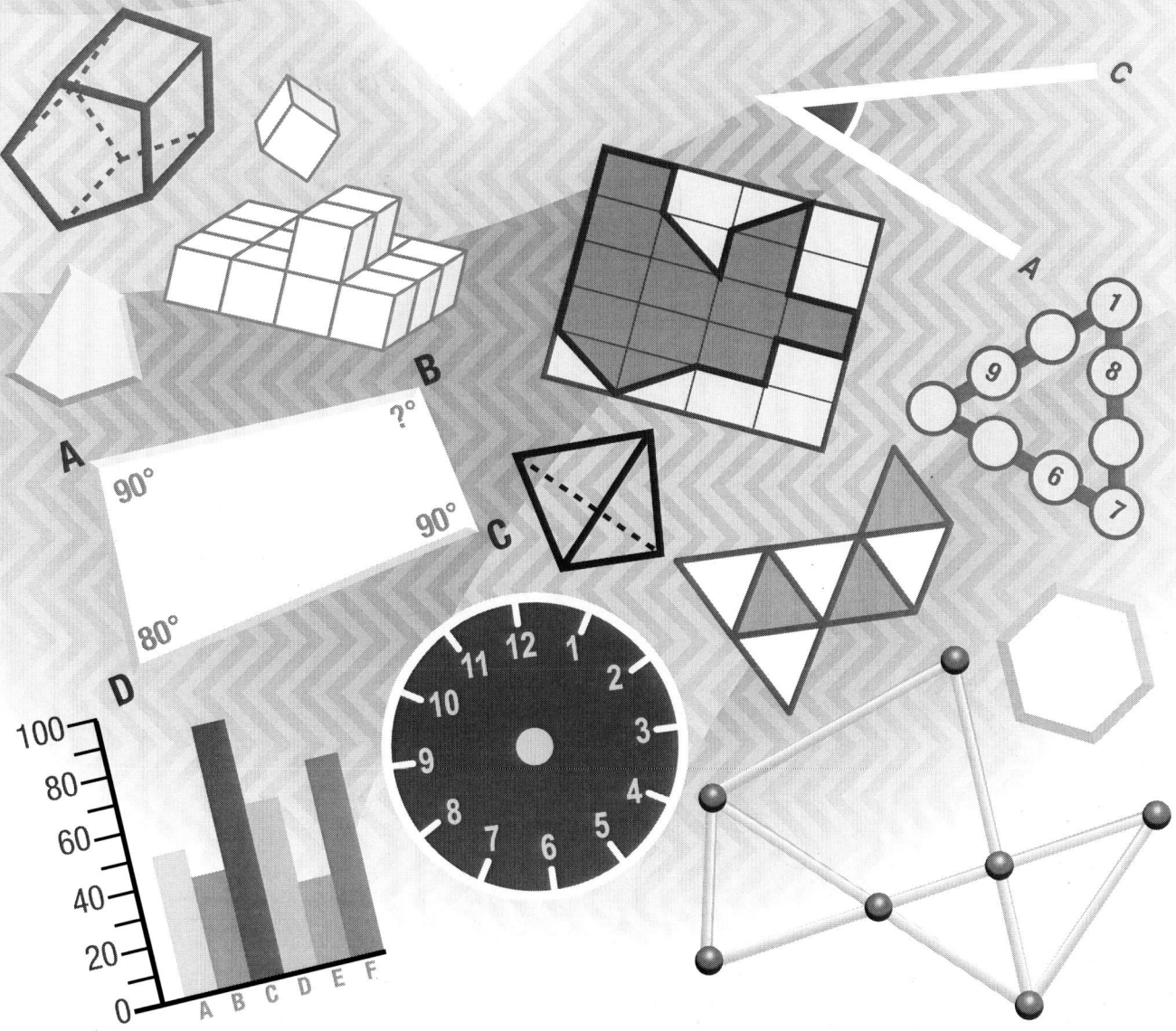

GEORGE MOORE

Mental Mathematics Practice Book 1

Copyright© George Moore 1995
Revised and reprinted by Prim-Ed Publishing® 2012
ISBN 978-1-84654-544-3

PR–9006

Titles available in this series:
Mental Mathematics Practice Book 1
Mental Mathematics Practice Book 2

This master may only be reproduced by the original purchaser for use with their class(es). The publisher prohibits the loaning or onselling of this master for the purposes of reproduction.

Copyright Notice

Blackline masters or copy masters are published and sold with a limited copyright. This copyright allows publishers to provide teachers and schools with a wide range of learning activities without copyright being breached. This limited copyright allows the purchaser to make sufficient copies for use within their own education institution. The copyright is not transferable, nor can it be onsold. Following these instructions is not essential but will ensure that you, as the purchaser, have evidence of legal ownership to the copyright if inspection occurs.

For your added protection in the case of copyright inspection, please complete the form below. Retain this form, the complete original document and the invoice or receipt as proof of purchase.

Name of Purchaser:
A M Banks

Date of Purchase:
_2/10/15_

Supplier:
_____

School Order# (if applicable):
_____

Signature of Purchaser:
_____

Internet websites

In some cases, websites or specific URLs may be recommended. While these are checked and rechecked at the time of publication, the publisher has no control over any subsequent changes which may be made to webpages. It is *strongly* recommended that the class teacher checks *all* URLs before allowing pupils to access them.

View all pages online

Website: http://www.prim-ed.com

Introduction

The **MENTAL MATHEMATICS PRACTICE** series is designed with the following features in mind:

1. **Comprehensive Coverage**

   Every book in the four book series contains:
   - 24 worksheets;
   - 24 revision worksheets;
   - answer sheets;
   - an extensive glossary of terms and symbols; and
   - class record/evaluation sheet.

2. **Wide-ranging Concepts**

   Every book in the **MENTAL MATHEMATICS PRACTICE** series includes hundreds of different problems covering many areas of the curriculum including number, algebra, space, shape, measures and data handling.

3. **Relevance**

   Every book covers a wide range of mathematical terms and symbols, which are subsequently described in the glossary. This makes them an excellent resource for developing and consolidating mathematical language.

4. **Practical**

   Every book provides revision sheets with similar kinds of problems to their corresponding worksheets but adopting a slightly greater degree of difficulty to reinforce the mathematical topics covered. Class record sheets provide the teacher with a single record for keeping track of each pupil's progress through this series.

Contents

Work Sets 1 to 24	1–24
Revision Sets 1 to 24	25–48
Glossary of Terms	49–51
Pupil Assessment Record	52–53
Answers	54–60

Which Book?

The MENTAL MATHEMATICS PRACTICE series has been written to meet curriculum and developmental requirements of children aged eight years through to eleven years. Individual children outside this age range will still have use for these activities, depending on their level of development.

The two books are progressive in difficulty.

Notes from the Author

These activities have been designed to stimulate interest in mathematics using a problem-solving format. Where many mental mathematics books provide a continuous list of basic algorithms intent on consolidating basic facts, this series provides the same concept or topic development and adds in another dimension which is problem solving.

This allows the books to be used as a supplementary resource to add to the already essential work involved with automatic response to basic problems.

Many of the concepts provided in the book allow for class and group discussion to ensure that the mathematical idea is fully understood as well as the introduction and use of many new mathematical terms.

The use of these books provide a multitude of applications in the classroom. These include group and partner work; evaluation of areas of weakness; challenging individual minds; remedial work by using earlier books in the series; and many more.

I have written this series to provide a new and challenging approach to mental maths that will both develop mathematical ideas and motivate young minds.

About the Author:

George Moore has been a practising classroom teacher for over 30 years, with experience in primary and secondary areas.
He has held teaching and promotional positions in the United Kingdom and Australia.

Set 1

1. Four tens + 23 = _____

2. Write the largest number you can with the figures 2, 1, 3 and 5.

    ____ ____ ____ ____

3. To the nearest centimetre, which line below is 4-cm long?

    (a) _____

    (b) _____

    (c) _____

    (d) _____

4. Shade the fraction ⅕ in one of these diagrams.

    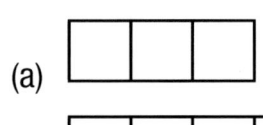

5. Complete the last basic number fact in the set below:

    9 x 4 = 36
    36 ÷ 4 = 9
    4 x 9 = 36

    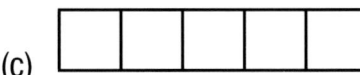

6. Write in figures five thousand and twelve:

    ____ ____ ____ ____

7. How many 1-cm cubes would you stack onto this grid to make a larger cube?

    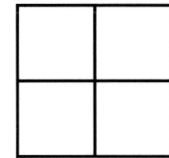

8. Think about the ½ and use your calculator to work out this sum:

    ½ of 96 = _____

9. Circle the earliest time shown on the digital clocks below:

10. ▼ ▼ □ ▲ ▲ □ ▼ ____ ____ ____

    Complete the pattern of shapes.

11. The shaded part is

    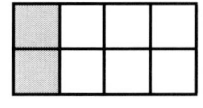

    (a) ¼   (b) ⅕
    (c) one part (d) one tenth.

12. An ant walked ____ cm from A to B on this network of paths:

    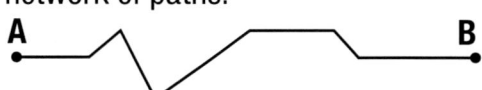

13. Use the number patterns to complete the last line.

    3 x 4 = 10 + 2
    3 x 5 = 12 + 3
    3 x 6 = 14 + 4
    3 x 7 = 16 + 5

    □ x □ = □ + □

14. An inside region is an interior area enclosed by a perimeter.

    ____ inside regions in this shape.

    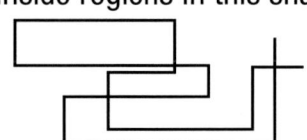

15. Fill in the missing numbers in this clockwise pattern.

    6, _, 24, 30, _, 42, _, _

Set 2

1. ☐ ÷ 4 = 5

2. I estimate the width of our classroom is _____ metres.

3. 37 rounded to the nearest 10 = _____.

4. Toffees are 5p each but if I buy a packet of ten for 35p I save myself _____ pence.

5. 5 x ☐ = 3 x 10

6. When zero is taken from a number the answer is always:
   (a) a zero,   (b) one,
   (c) less than the number,
   (d) the same as the number.

7. This shape below is divided into:
   (a) thirds
   (b) equal parts
   (c) 3 unequal parts
   (d) quarters
   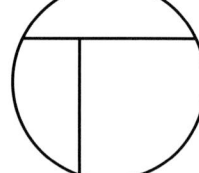

8. XX – XV = _____
   Give the answer in Roman numerals.

9. The area of shape A is:
   (a) 2 x shape B's area.
   (b) 3 x shape B's area.
   (c) 4 x shape B's area.
   (d) 6 x shape B's area.
   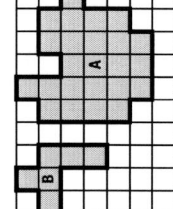

10. There are 7 intersections in shape A, and _____ intersections in shape B.
    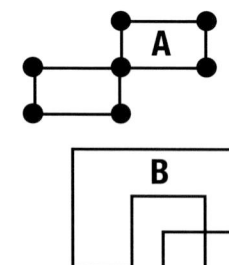

11.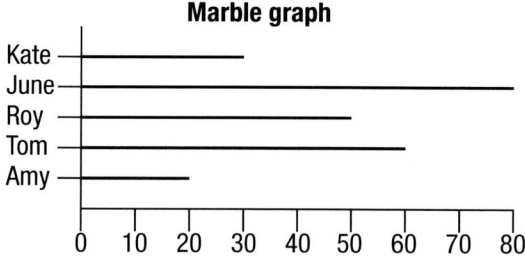
    Marble graph

    Tom has _____ times as many marbles as Amy but only 10 more than _____ on this bar graph.

12. These are two arrays for the number 6. Draw two arrays for the number 4 below:
    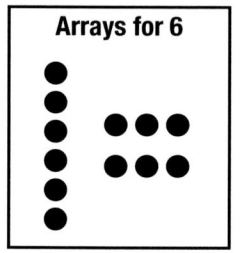 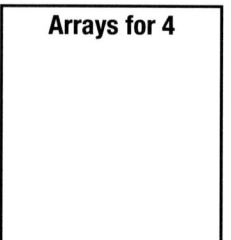

13. The diameter of a circle is twice its radius. The radius of this circle is _____ mm (use a ruler).
    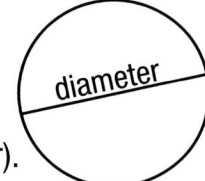

14. This cube has ☐ faces and ☐ edges.
    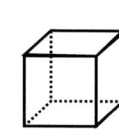

15.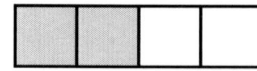
    halves
    quarters

    This diagram shows that the fraction ½ is the same as the fraction .

Set 3

1. Shade in the multiples of 3.

    | 3 | 4 | 5 | 6 | 7 | 8 | 9 | 10 | 11 | 12 |

2. If you halve an even number the answer is:
    (a) always odd
    (b) always even
    (c) odd or even
    (d) not odd or even

3.
   Put a cross in grid square (2,C) and colour in grid square (4,A).

4. Use the halving and doubling pattern to find the missing numbers:

    40 x 10 = 400
    20 x 20 = 400
    10 x 40 = 400
    ☐ x ☐ = 400

5. Julie is _____ cm tall.

6.
   Complete the next 2 shapes in this repeating pattern.

7.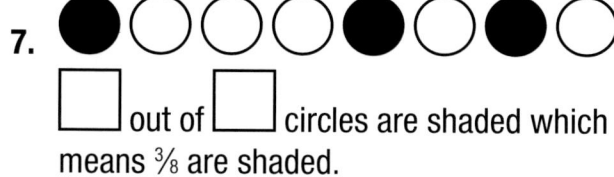
   ☐ out of ☐ circles are shaded which means ⅜ are shaded.

8. This is a closed curve with one intersection. Draw a closed curve with 2 intersections in the box.

9. Draw a line twice as long as line 'A' and then divide the new line into 4 equal lengths (ruler needed).

    A _____

10. I throw two dice and a 6 and a 3 come up. My next throw will be:
    (a) a 6 and a 3   (b) two 6's
    (c) I can't tell   (d) two 3's.

11. 400 + 27 units =

12. 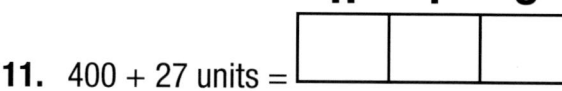 = 24

    The missing number in the square is 3 times bigger than each number in the triangles.

13.
    Use the addition pattern to complete the missing numbers.

    | 8 | 1 | 6 |
    | 3 | | |
    | 4 | | 2 |

14. Join 2 points on the parallel sides and divide the trapezium into 2 congruent (equal) shapes (ruler needed).

15. Concentric circles have the same centre. The width of the second largest concentric circle shown is _____ mm.

Set 4

1. The answer to an even number X an even number:
   (a) is always odd
   (b) is odd or even
   (c) is always even
   (d) always ends in 2

2.
   The best number sentence for this diagram is:
   (a) 2 + 4 = 6   (b) 3 x 2 = 6
   (c) 8 - 2 = 6   (d) 3 + 3 = 6

3. Complete the next 2 numbers in the pattern:
   5   8   10   6   15   4   ___   ___

4. I bought 20 marbles and half as many stamps. The marbles were 10 for 50p and stamps were 10p each.

   Total cost = £_____

5. Join the dots to form squares. The area of shape ☐ is 3 x the area of shape ☐.
   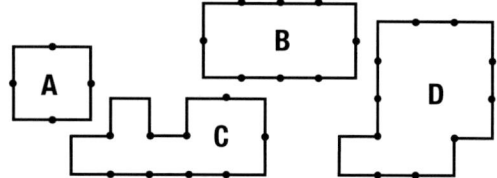

6. Complete the last line by following the pattern:
   47p x 10 = £4.70
   23p x 10 = £2.30
   68p x 10 = £6.80

   76p x 10 = £_____

7. Draw the pattern in box B after box A has had a ¼ clockwise turn.
   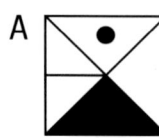 

8. 6 + 6 + 6 gives the same answer as:
   (a) 3 + 9 + 3   (b) (6 x 2) + (6 x 1)
   (c) (6 + 6) x 3   (d) 6 x 6 x 6

9. Show 1500 hours on the clock. The hour hand is shorter.

10. ☐ + ☐ + ☐ + 5 = 65
    The missing numbers are all different and are all multiples of 10.

11. This hexagonal prism has ☐ edges.

12. Think about the ½ and use your calculator to work out this sum:
    72 x ½ x 24 = _____

13. Draw one line to divide this shape into 2 congruent (equal) parts. You will need to measure distances with your ruler.

14.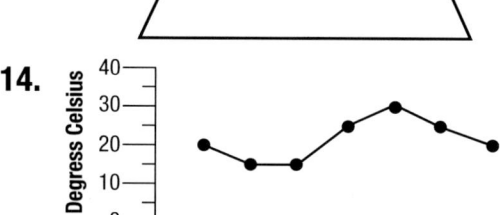
    The difference between the highest and lowest temperatures during this week was
    _____ degrees Celsius.

15. Shade in the balloon which contains a number that can be divided exactly by 4, 5 and 10.

Set 5

1. The answer to 294 x 7 is:
   (a) 1664   (b) 2058
   (c) 2116   (d) 1824

2. Use the patterns to complete the last line:
   (3 x 5) + 1 = 10 + 6
   (3 x 5) + 3 = 10 + 8
   (3 x 5) + 5 = 10 + 10
   (3 x 5) + 7 = 10 + 12
   (☐ x ☐) + ☐ = ☐ + ☐

3. 27 x ☐ = 0

4. These are the 4 arrays for the number 6. Draw all the arrays for the number 8.
   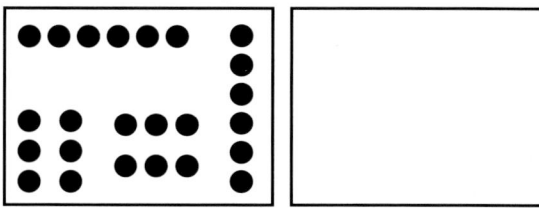

5. A _____   B _____
   C _____ D _____
   Line B is ☐ cm shorter than line C but ☐ cm longer than line A or line D.

6. Circle the numbers which can be divided into 2 equal whole numbers:
   17   8   21   26   13   12   5

7. 2 m 32 cm = 2.32 m
   5 m 3 cm = 5.03 m
   so 8 m 72 cm = _____ m
   7 m 5 cm = _____ m

8. How many times bigger is the underlined 3 than the other 3 in the number 23̲43?
   (a) 30 times   (b) 300 times
   (c) 10 times   (d) 100 times

9. £5 + 20p 10p 5p £2 20p 50p
   = £ _____

10. Complete the next 2 arrow diagrams in this pattern:
    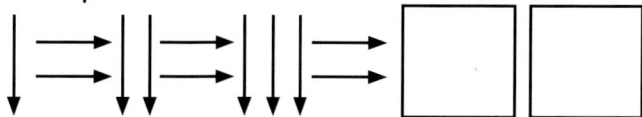

11. Put down the 20th letter, the 15th letter and the second from last letter of the alphabet to make a word:
    ☐ ☐ ☐

12. Use your calculator to multiply the product of 2 and 9 by two thousand one hundred and one. Turn the calculator upside down and write the word in the display window:
    _____

13. The number of small cubes in this diagram is
    _____.

14. Move the dot 2 squares east, 3 squares southwest, one square south, and 4 squares east. Show the dot's new square.

15. To find the area of shape A you would:
    (a) count only whole squares
    (b) multiply length by width
    (c) count all whole squares and half squares
    (d) count only the half squares and double them

Set 6

1. Four thousands + 14 = _____

2. All square numbers can be arranged into a:
   (a) rectangle   (b) cube
   (c) square   (d) circle

3. Shade in the notes and coins needed to buy a £6.75 book:

   | £10 | £5 | 10p | £1 | 5p | £2 | 20p | 50p |

4.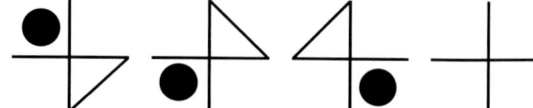

   Complete the next shape in the rotating pattern.

5. 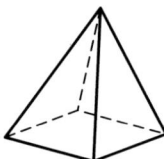 How many corners (vertices) on this pyramid with a square base?

   Vertices = _____

6. Round 403 and 291 to the nearest hundred and find the sum of your 2 answers:

   Sum = _____

7.  The second tallest flower is _____ mm high.

8. Circle the smallest number:
   2436   3462   2463
   2643   2346   2634

9. A circle's radius is half its diameter. This circle's diameter is _____ mm

10. Complete the next 3 counting numbers:
    996, 997, 998, _____ , _____ , _____

11. _____ g + _____ g + 500 g = 1 kg.

12.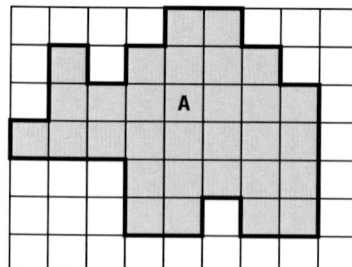

    The perimeter of shape A on this ½-cm grid is _____ cm.

13.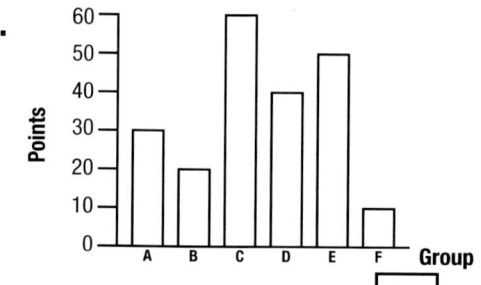

    On this block graph group ☐ scored 30 points more than group ☐ and 10 more than group D.

14. 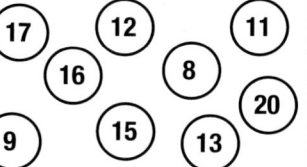 Shade in the 2 circles which total (add up to) 30.

15. _____ small cubes have to be added to this shape to make a 3-cm cube.

    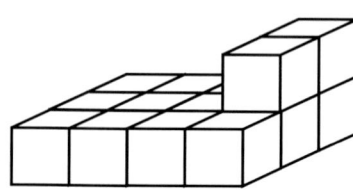

Set 7

1. 24 x 10 =
   24 x 100 =
   24 x 1000 =

TT	T	H	T	U
		2	4	0
	2	4	0	0

2.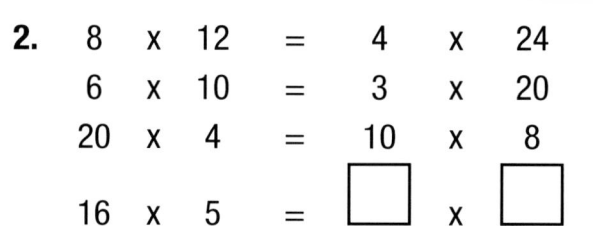

   Look at the doubling and halving pattern to find the missing numbers.

3. Circle the numbers which will be even numbers when they are doubled:

   6   ½   3   1½
   2½   5   3½   21

4. In one minute I could skip about:
   (a) 10 times   (b) 50 times
   (c) 400 times   (d) 5 times

5. **Football** (4 12 5) **Hockey**

   This Venn diagram shows that 17 pupils like hockey. How many like football?
   _____

6. 80 cm + 40 cm + 30 cm = _____ m

7. A B C D E

   Shade in the shape that is different from the others.

8.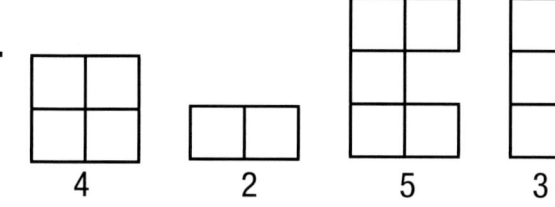
   4   2   5   3
   Shade in the square number in the above shapes.

9. £1 is made up of: four 20p coins + one 10p coin + _____ 5p coins.

10. To find the perimeter of this shape (a closed curve) I would use:
    (a) my ruler
    (b) a trundle wheel
    (c) a ruler and cotton
    (d) a compass

11. Use your ruler to measure and then shade in the 2 shapes (polygons) with the same perimeter.

12. ☐ lots of 19 = 133 (Use a calculator!)

13. **November**

S	M	T	W	T	F	S
			1	2	3	4
5	6	7	8	9	10	11
12	13	14	15	16	17	18
19	20	21	22	23	24	25
26	27	28	29	30		

    Using the number patterns circle the date which is 14 days after 8 November.

14. ○○○○○○○○
    Shade in the fourth circle after the centre circle above.

15. Complete the last shape of the rotating pattern below:

    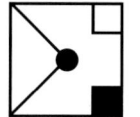   

Set 8

1. VIII + II + I = ☐

2.  Join some dots to make a right-angled triangle.

3. The answer to the sum 3 x 1 x 3 x 5 is 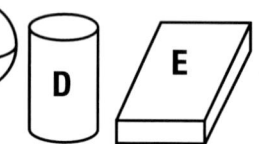 (shade your answer).

4. Complete the next 2 numbers in the series:

   AB12, CD10, EF8, GH6, _____, _____

5.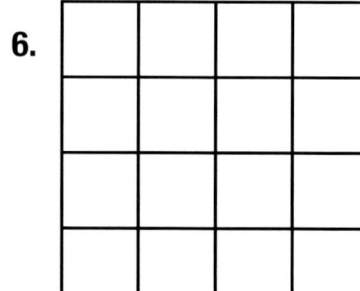

   Shade the sphere and the cylinder.

6. On this 1-cm grid draw a shape with a perimeter of 8 cm. Do not draw a square.

7. The fraction shaded is:
   (a) ½ (b) ⅔
   (c) ¾ (d) ²⁄₆
   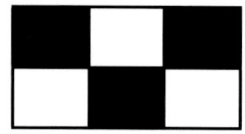

8. Circle the odd numbers:

   7, 12, 24, 37, 276, 359, 1021

9.

   Tim   Amy   May   Rod

   _____ and _____ are taller than _____, who is taller than _____, who is the shortest.

10. Eight hundred – 500 = _____.

11. All even numbers can be divided exactly by:
    (a) 10   (b) 6
    (c) 2   (d) 4

12.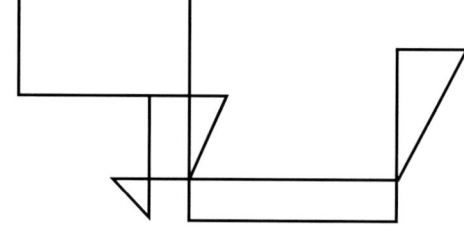

    Three and 4 will divide into 24 exactly so it is shaded. Shade other numbers which can be divided by 3 and 4.

13. An inside region is an interior area enclosed by a perimeter. This shape has one outside region and _____ inside regions.

14. A _____ B _____ C _____
    D _____ E _____ F _____

    I could use lines ☐B and ☐F and ☐ and ☐ to make a rectangle.

15. Ann planned to save 50p a week for 8 weeks. In the 5th week she saved twice her usual amount. How much did she save in the 8 weeks?

    Savings = £_____

Set 9

1. Complete the pattern of square numbers below:

   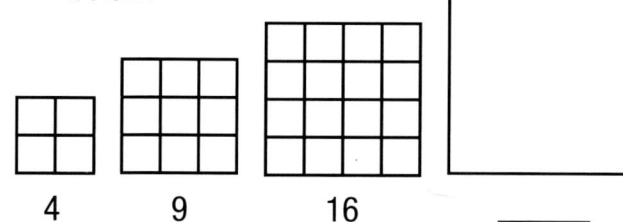

   4   9   16   ___

2. If you rearrange the digits of 185 you can make the numbers:

   158, 851, 815, 518 and ☐.

3. Draw hands on the clock to show 11.10 a.m. The hour hand is shorter.

4. 30 + 700 + 2 =

H	T	U

5. The difference between 10 and 17 is the same as the difference between:
   (a) 17 and 11   (b) 15 and 21
   (c) 9 and 16   (d) 8 and 18

6.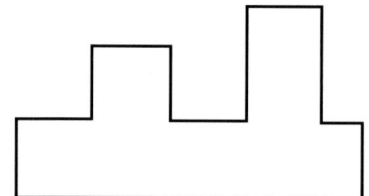

   I estimate the perimeter of this shape is about:
   (a) 30 cm   (b) 8 cm
   (c) 16 cm   (d) 22 cm

7.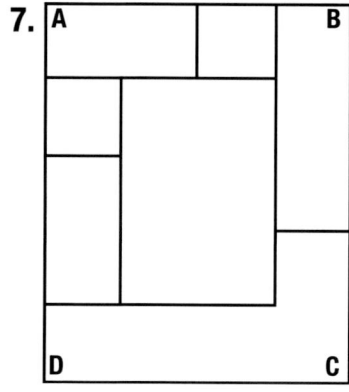

   Continue the lines in shape ABCD to divide it into squares.

   Its area = _____ squares (cm²)

8. A _____

   Half of line A is _____ cm or _____ mm. Use a ruler.

9. In a class of 28, ten children were at sports practice and half of the rest at choir practice. How many children were left in the classroom?

   _____ children.

10. If you double the length of each side of shape A, the new shape has _____ times as many squares in its area.

11. (5 x 12) − 10 = 50
    (4 x 12) − 8 = 40
    (3 x 12) − 6 = 30
    (2 x 12) − 4 = 20
    (☐ x ☐) − ☐ = ☐

12. ☐ + ☐ + ☐ = 1

13. The numbers in the boxes are all multiples of 4. Write the missing multiple of 4 which is less than 40.

8	36	12
16		4
24	28	20

14.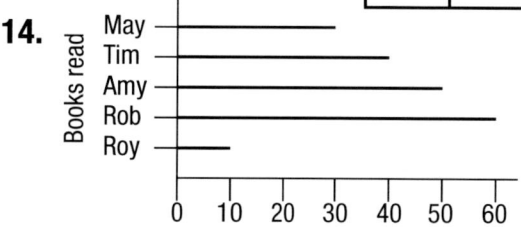

    This bar graph shows that _____ has read four times as many books as _____.

15. The total length of all edges in this cuboid = _____ cm.

    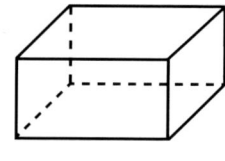

Set 10

1. 2 x 10 [>] [<] [=] 4 x 8

   Shade in the box which makes a true maths sentence.

2. 200 g x ☐ = 1 kg

3.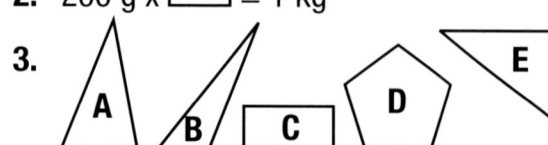

   Shade in the shape which has only one right angle.

4. An odd number + another odd number always gives an [ODD] [EVEN] number. Shade in your answer.

5. I estimate my teacher's height to be _____ cm.

6. Circle the objects which are longer than one metre:

   pencil   broom   tray
   bed   bat   book

7.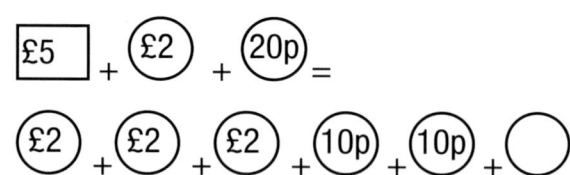

   Draw the rest of the arrows to complete this mapping diagram by using the relation sign in the box.

8. A rectangle's length is twice its width. Its perimeter is 24 cm. Its measurements are:
   (a) 4 and 2 cm   (b) 6 and 3 cm
   (c) 10 and 5 cm   (d) 8 and 4 cm

9. Circle the fraction which is less than ½:

   ⅞   ¾   ⁵⁄₁₀   ⅜   ⁶⁄₁₂

10. Use the number patterns to complete the last line:

    (12 x 5) – 0 = 60
    (12 x 6) – 2 = 70
    (12 x 7) – 4 = 80
    (12 x 8) – 6 = 90
    (☐ x ☐) – ☐ = ☐

11.

    Colour in the right-angled triangles in this diagram.

12. David June Amy Peter

    _____ is the shortest as he is shorter than _____ and _____, who are both taller than _____.

13. Complete this money maths sentence:

    £5 + £2 + 20p =
    £2 + £2 + £2 + 10p + 10p + ○

14. | | 4 x table | 5 x table |
    |---|---|---|
    | Odd | | 5 |
    | Even | 12 | |

    Use the numbers **less than 20** that fit into the Carrol diagram. Two have been done for you.

15. The longest side of this 6-sided shape is ____ cm or ____ mm longer than its shortest side (ruler needed).

Set 11

1. Any even number divided by itself gives an answer which is:
   (a) odd or even (b) even
   (c) not odd or even (d) odd

2.  Colour in one semi-circle in this diagram.

3. ≠ > < = ÷
   Use one of these symbols to make this maths sentence true: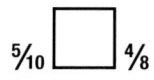

4.

   Circle the digital clock which shows 4 p.m.

5. Put these fractions in order from smallest to largest: ½   ¼   ¹⁄₁₀

   _____

6. If two odd numbers are added to any even number, the answer is always:
   (a) correct (b) even
   (c) odd (d) odd or even

7. A tennis ball weighs about:
   (a) 2 g (b) 50 g
   (c) 2 kg (d) 5 kg

8.
   Circle the shape which has one line of symmetry.

9. 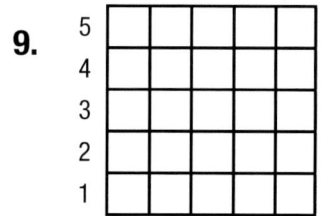 Shade in grid square (2, 5) and put a cross in grid square (4, 3).

10. How many small cubes would I have if I doubled the number in this shape? _____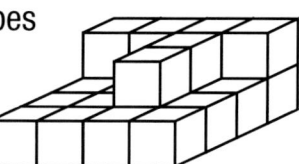

11. Share £22 among John, Mary and Rhonda so Mary gets 3 times as much as John and twice as much as Rhonda.

    Mary's share   = £ _____
    John's share   = £ _____
    Rhonda's share = £ _____

12. Draw 2 lines to divide this shape into 3 congruent (equal) rectangles. You need your ruler to measure.

    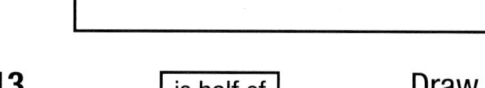

13. Draw the rest of the arrows to complete this mapping diagram.

    is half of
    2½ 3½ 13 0.5 17
    7 26 34 5 1 14

14. Shade in the number which is the product of 2 other numbers in the circle.

    24 5 18 7 32 36
    37 31 4 40 6 21

15. Using only the numbers up to twenty fill in the Venn diagram.

    multiples of 2   multiples of 3

    2   3

Set 12

1. 2 x 12 = ☐ + ☐ + ☐

   The missing numbers are all the same.

2. Follow the pattern to find the missing numbers:

   | 3000 | + | 300 | + ☐ + ☐ = 3333

3. To walk around a netball court would take me about:
   (a) 10 mins (b) 20 mins
   (c) 1 min   (d) 5 mins

4. There are ____ different kinds of shapes in this diagram.

5. Colour in the shapes which will **tessellate** (fit together without gaps between the shapes).

6. Rounding 358 to the nearest ten is:
   (a) 350 (b) 300
   (c) 360 (d) 355

7. The above tallies show:
   (a) 8 + 15   (b) 10 + 15
   (c) 4 + 6   (d) 10 + 18

8. I have £24. Tim has twice as much and Ann has £8 less than my amount. How much do we have altogether?

   £_____

9. There are no [ODD] [EVEN] multiples of 4 because 4 is an [ODD] [EVEN] number. Shade in your answers.

10. If I draw straight lines to join all the corners (vertices) in this pentagon (5-sided shape) the number of small triangles formed would be:
    (a) 8 (b) 12 (c) 9 (d) 10

11. 50 + 100 + 50 + 50 + 100 + 50 + 200 + 50 + 200

    How many fifties do we have if we add the above numbers? _____

12. The cross is in the [INSIDE] [OUTSIDE] region of this shape and the dot is in the [INSIDE] [OUTSIDE] region. Shade in your answers.

13. **August**

S	M	T	W	T	F	S
		1	2	3	4	5	6
7	8	9	10	11	12	13
14	15	16	17	18	19	20
21	22	23	24	25	26	27
28	29	30	31			

    The total number of Tuesdays and Fridays in this month is _____.

14. The total length of the **vertical** lines in this shape is _____ cm or _____ mm.

15. There are 24 children in a class. Thirteen like maths and spelling. Five like spelling only and 19 like maths. Show this information on the diagram.

    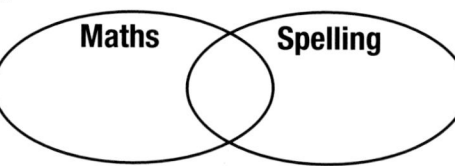

Set 13

1. 40 × 7 ☐ 7 × 40
   Use the correct symbol (≠ > = <) to make the maths sentence true.

2. 6 squared (6²) − 6 = _____

3. Complete the series:
   2:03, 2:05, 2:07, 2:09, _____

4. Write all the odd prime numbers < 20 in the boxes:
   ☐ ☐ ☐ ☐ ☐ ☐ ☐

5. 1½ km − 1000 m = _____

6. $\frac{9}{10} - \frac{4}{10} = \frac{3}{10} + \frac{\square}{10}$

7. ☐9☐ × ☐2☐ × ☐ = 18

8. Circle the 2 solid shapes (polyhedra) which have the same number of edges.
   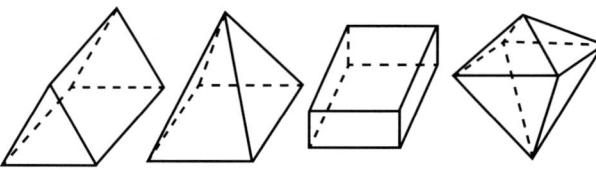

9. Round 2571 to the nearest 100. _____

10. 5 × 37 = (5 × ☐) + (5 × 7).

11. Draw a tally for 22:
    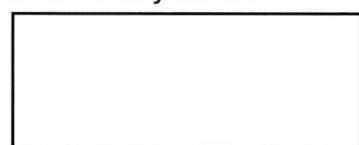

12. Circle the right angle (90°).

13. In 5 hours this digital clock will show _____.

14. With a coin I throw heads, then tails, then tails again. My next throw will be:
    (a) a head   (b) a tail
    (c) can't tell   (d) neither

15. Use the patterns to complete the columns.
    5 × 3 = 10 + 5
    5 × 30 = 100 + 50
    5 × 300 = 1 000 + 500
    5 × ____ = ____ + ____

16. A diagonal is a straight line joining two opposite corners.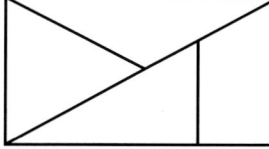
    The length of the rectangle's diagonal is ____ cm or ____ mm (ruler needed).

17. Shaded area ☐ is double shaded area ☐.

    A 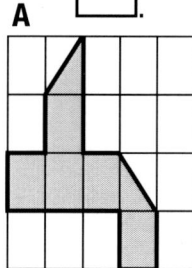   B 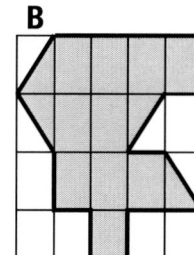   C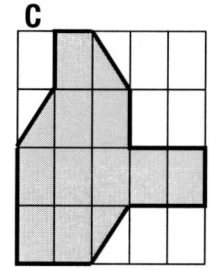

18. The area of any shape is:
    (a) its length × its width
    (b) the distance round it
    (c) the amount of surface it covers
    (d) twice the number of its sides

19. 2.5 metres > 205 cm. True or false?

20.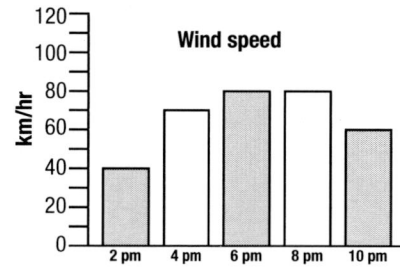
    Wind speed at 4 pm = _____ km/hr

Set 14

1. Write 7 2 0 8 in words. _____
2. 5m 87cm to the nearest metre = ____m.
3. $\frac{8}{8} < \frac{10}{10}$. True or false?
4. 1000 = 10 x ☐ x 10.
5. The number of one-centimetre cubes in this solid shape = _____.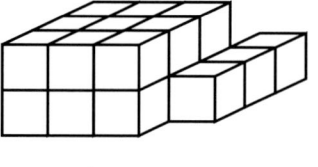
6. This tally of 100 ml containers totals _____ml.
7. A _____
   B _____
   C _____
   D _____
   Line ☐ is 2 cm longer than line ☐.
8. Complete the last row by using the patterns.
   15 ÷ 5 = 3
   150 ÷ 5 = 30
   1 500 ÷ 5 = 300
   ____ ÷ 5 = ____
9. Round the numbers in the boxes to complete the maths sentence.
   ☐21 x ☐38 ≈ ____ x ____ = 800.
10. 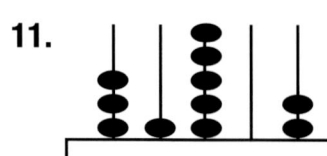 The shaded area contains ☐/8.
11. 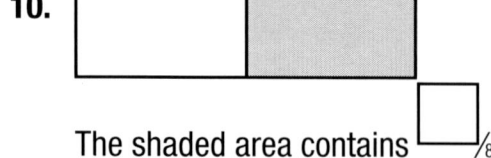 The number shown on the abacus is _____.

12. An isosceles ▲ has 2 congruent sides. Shade in the isosceles ▲ below (check with a ruler).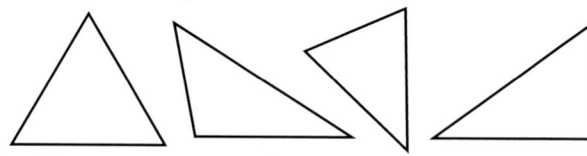
13. The arrow turns clockwise through 270° (90° + 90° + 90°). Show its new position.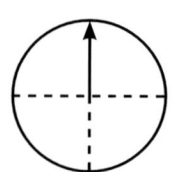
14. Tickets to a school zoo trip were £3 each. £72 was collected. How many pupils went? _____
15. 3 x (☐ + 1) = 15.
16. This Venn diagram shows the results of a class survey.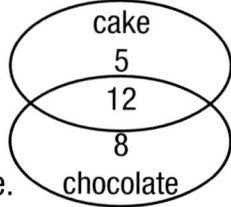
    _____ liked chocolate.
    _____ liked both.
    _____ liked only cake.
17. 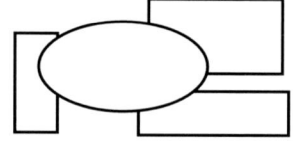 Pupil ____ had 3 times as many marks as pupil ____.
18. How many 2 cm diagonals can be ruled in this shape.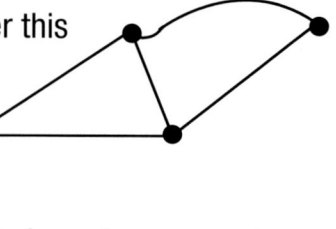
19. Can you travel over this network of paths without going over the same path twice?
20. Circle the objects below whose mass is measured in grams.
    letter | bed | car | pencil | leaf

Set 15

1. 30 × ☐ = 600

2.
   ```
        ☐  4  ☐
             × 6
     ─────────
      4  ☐  5  8
   ```

3. Draw the next 2 shapes in this series.

    ____ ____

4. X V I I + I V = _____
   Answer in Roman numerals.

5. A _____
   B _____   C _____
           D _____

   Line A is _____ cm longer than the shortest line.

6. My friend's mass is measured in:
   (a) grams   (b) tonnes
   (c) kilograms   (d) litres.

7. Colour in the 3-dimensional solid shape.

   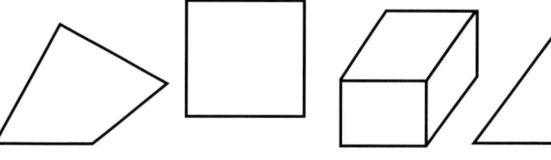

8. Take the sum of 3, 14 and 20 away from 50.   ☐ =

9. (4 + 6) + 2 = 4 + (☐ + 2)

10. Write the odd composite numbers less than 20 in the boxes. ☐☐

11. How many small cubes would you put on this grid to make a large cube?

    _____ cubes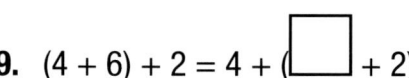

12. There are 2 black queens in a pack of 52 cards. So I have a 2 in 52 chance (or 1 in 26) of drawing a black queen. What is the chance of drawing an ace?
    (a) 1 in 52   (b) 1 in 26
    (c) 4 in 52   (d) 1 in 33

13. $3^4 = 3 \times 3 \times 3 \times 3$
    $4^3 = 4 \times 4 \times 4$
    $2^5 =$

14. How many regions are there in this network of paths? Remember, there is an outside region too!

    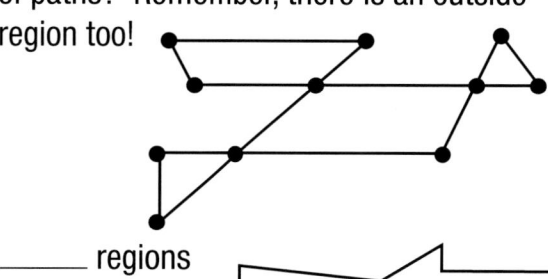

    _____ regions

15. Draw in any line (axis) of symmetry you can see in this shape.

    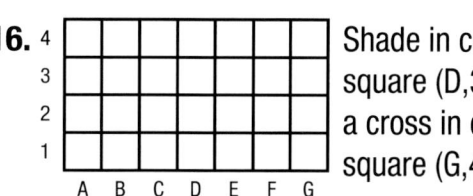

16.  Shade in coordinate square (D,3) and put a cross in coordinate square (G,4).

17. In ½ an hour the time on this clock will be:
    (a) 4:40 p.m.   (b) 1430
    (c) 12:30 p.m.   (d) 1630

    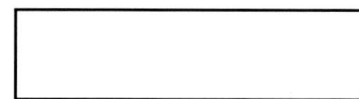

18. Draw a line 3-cm long in the box and put a red dot in the centre of it.

19. Colour the shapes which will tessellate.

    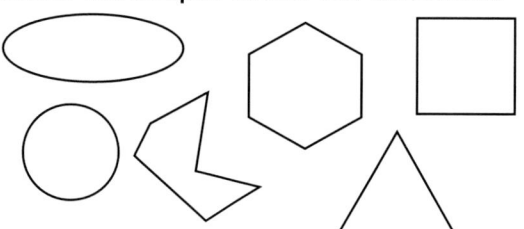

20. The estimated perimeter (circumference) of this circle is

    _____ cm.

Set 16

1. The total value of the underlined digit in the number 34_21.6 is:
   (a) 4   (b) 4000   (c) 400   (d) 40

2. Write the smallest possible number with the digits 5, 3, 2, 4, 8. _____

3. The common numeral for 4000 + 200 + 7 is: _____

4.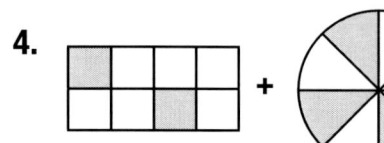

   Total fraction shaded is:
   (a) $\frac{5}{16}$ (b) $\frac{5}{12}$ (c) $\frac{5}{8}$ (d) $\frac{5}{5}$

5. 2.099 > 2.1. True or false?

6. Look at the pattern between rows A and B and complete the grid.

A	2	4	12	10	0
B	5	9	25		

7. Show the number 4023 on the abacus.

   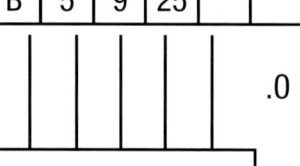

8. 195 + 202 ≈ (is approximately):
   (a) 500   (b) 300   (c) 400   (d) 200

9. A 10-year-old girl could run 100 metres in:
   (a) 25 sec.   (b) 10 sec.
   (c) 5 sec.   (d) 8 sec.

10. Measure with your ruler and then shade in the shapes with the same perimeter.

11. Circle the set of numbers between 220 and 250 from the list below.

    217, 202, 223, 253, 241, 221

12. Measure with your ruler and divide this trapezium into 3 congruent triangles.

    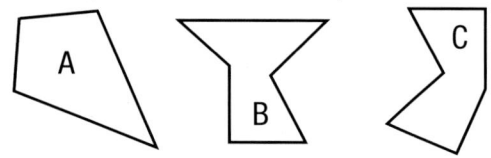

13. Circle the array which shows an odd number.

14. Complete the maths sentences. The missing numbers are the same in each line.

    □ × □ × □ = 6
    □ + □ + □ = 6

15. Using only the numbers 30, 6 and 5 complete the different basic number facts below.

    30 ÷ 5 = 6
    __ ÷ __ = __
    __ × __ = __
    __ × __ = __

16. In this network the shortest path is between points (intersections) □ and □ (ruler needed).

    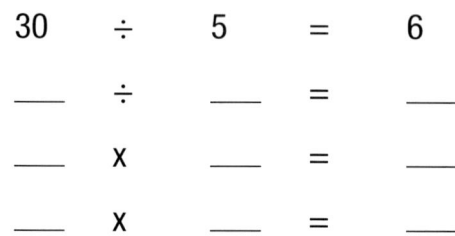

17. Roy puts £15 a week into his bank account. After 5 weeks he's only drawn out £20. How much is left in his account? £_____

18. Circle the 2 clocks showing the same time.

19. Can you draw along all the paths in this network without going over the same path twice (is it traversable)? _____

20. Rule arrows in this mapping diagram. The pairs must agree with the relation sign in the box.

    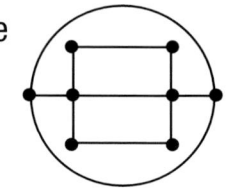

    is a multiple of

Set 17

1. The number which is 15 less than 500 is _____.

2. True or false?

   3 x 5 x 2 = 2 x 3 x 5.

3. Circle the whole number:

   5/10   3/12   10/10   9/12   5/8   1/8

4. Complete the series:

   AB9, CD7, EF5, _____, _____

5. Points ☐ and ☐ are 2½ cm apart (ruler needed).

6. Put the composite numbers between 10 and 20 in the boxes.

   ☐ ☐ ☐ ☐ ☐

7. Using only the digits 2, 7, and 4 write the numbers greater than 300.

   (a) _____   (b) _____
   (c) _____   (d) _____

8. We would measure the distance around a tennis court in:

   (a) metres   (b) cm   (c) mm   (d) km

9. The time shown is:

   (a) 9:10   (b) 9:45
   (c) 8:50   (d) 8:40

10. 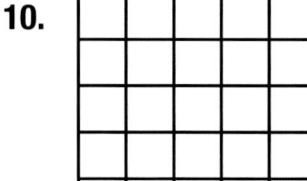 Shade in a square which does not touch a square on the perimeter of the grid.

11.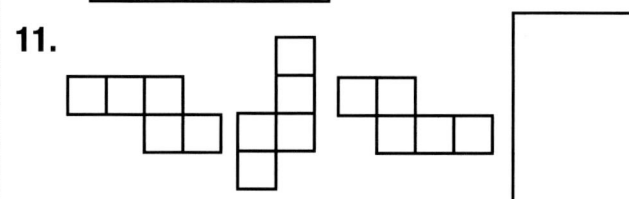

    Follow the rotating (turning) pattern and draw the next pentomino in the box.

12. Complete the missing numbers on the number line. No improper fractions (e.g. 13/10) can be used.

    2/10   5/10   8/10   ☐   1 4/10   ☐

13. Colour in the shapes with the same number of vertices.

14. I double the sum of 4 and ☐ and the answer is 14. Put in the missing number.

15. In which direction would you travel if you went from the dot to grid point (C,3), then to point (D,2)?

    (a) NW   (b) SE   (c) NE   (d) SW

    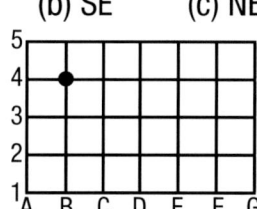

16. ☐ x ☐ x ☐ = 30

    The missing numbers are 3 different prime numbers.

17. True or false?

    3 x 0 x 8 x 6 > 2 x 1 x 1

18. Colour the shape which has one horizontal line (axis) of symmetry.

    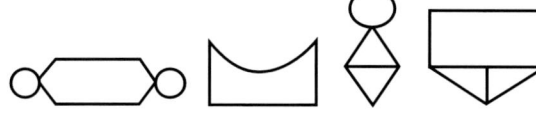

19.  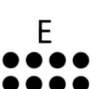 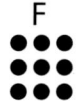 Circle the arrays which show square numbers.

20. 3 x ½ km = _____ metres.

Set 18

1. The total value of the 6 in 2365 is:
   (a) 600   (b) 6   (c) 60   (d) 6000

2. $9.35 = 9 + \square/10 + \square/100$

3. A cylinder is made up of 2 circles and a:
   (a) square or rectangle   (b) triangle
   (c) semicircle   (d) diamond

4. The lowest common multiple of 5, 6 and 10 is _____.

5. Circle the dot which is 2 cm from the left side of the box and 2 cm from the top.

6. Look at the patterns and complete the bottom line.
   (3 x 1000) – 3 = 2997
   (4 x 1000) – 4 = 3996
   (5 x 1000) – 5 = 4995
   (6 x 1000) – 6 = 5994
   (☐ x ☐) – ☐ = ☐

7. You would measure your height in:
   (a) mm   (b) km   (c) cm   (d) kg

8. Colour in the shape with the least number of vertices and the shape with the most.

9. Using only the numerals 1 to 9, fill in the missing numbers so that the sides of the triangle have the same total.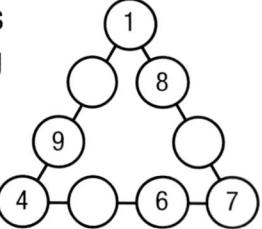

10. Shade in the shape with the most right angles.
    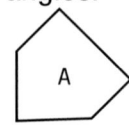 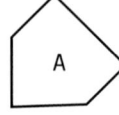 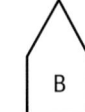 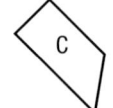 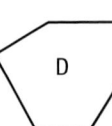

11. Two bats and three balls cost £33. The balls are £3 each and the bats each cost the same price. Cost of a bat = £_____ .

12. The difference between the longest and the shortest line segment is ☐ cm or ☐ mm.
    A _____ B _____
    C _____
    D _____

13. Jenny is _____ tall.

14. X X V I + ☐ = X X X I.
    Give your answer in Roman numerals.

15. Town A is _____ km from Town B.
    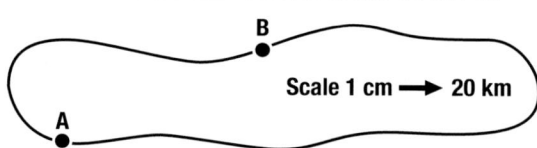

16. David ate 6/10 of his chocolate bar. He then gave away 1/4 of the pieces left. Shade in the fraction given away.
    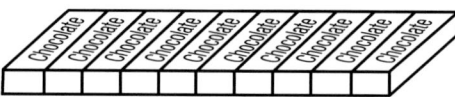

17. Circle the shaded fractions which are the same.
    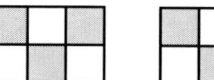 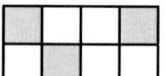 

18. Circle the time which is about 7 p.m.
    18:30   18:55   06:50   18:05

19. If you stacked 3 of these shapes on top of each other you would have a:
    (a) cube   (b) cylinder
    (c) square
    (d) rectangular prism

20. On this 1-cm grid the area shaded = _____ cm².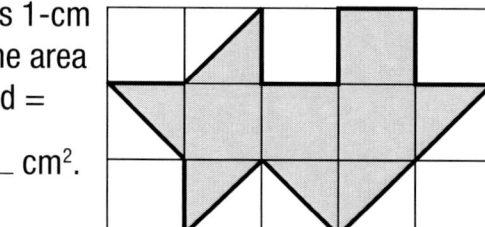

Set 19

1. (13 × 3) − ☐ = 39

2. If the last 2 digits of these dates can be exactly divided by 4, then the date is a leap year. Circle the leap years below.
   1952, 1963, 1987, 1908, 1992

3. Write the multiples of 4 between 10 and 30 in the boxes.
   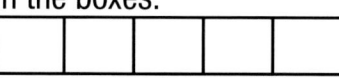

4. 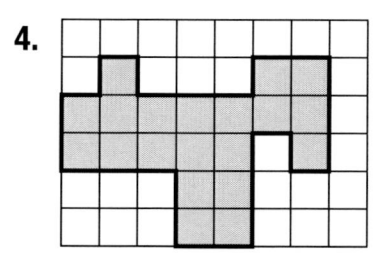 The perimeter of the shaded shape on this ½ cm grid
   is: _____ cm or
   _____ mm

5. Put these decimal fractions in ascending order (from least to largest).
   2.22, 0.2, 2.02, 2.0, 2.2
   _____, _____, _____, _____, _____

6.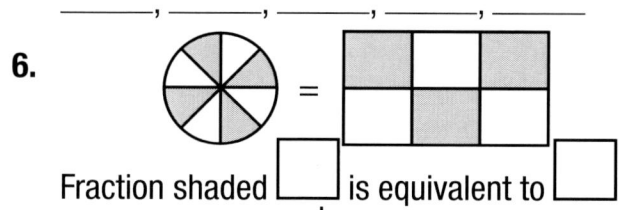
   Fraction shaded ☐ is equivalent to ☐ .

7.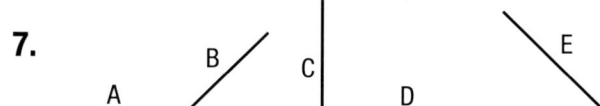
   Circle the horizontal line segment which is 15 mm long.

8. Shade in the clock which shows 1400 hours.

9. A rounding estimate of the answer to 21 + 32 + 49 is:
   (a) 80   (b) 90   (c) 100   (d) 200

10. The place value of the underlined digit in 73<u>6</u>.5 is:
    (a) 100s   (b) tenths   (c) tens   (d) units

11. What is the largest number that can be written with only 3 digits? _____

12. ☐ Measure and then draw lines in the rectangle to show it has an area of 6 cm².

13. I estimate the width of our classroom is ⟦LONGER⟧ ⟦SHORTER⟧ than its height. Shade in your answer.

14. There are 5 tetrominoes. Draw the fifth one in the box.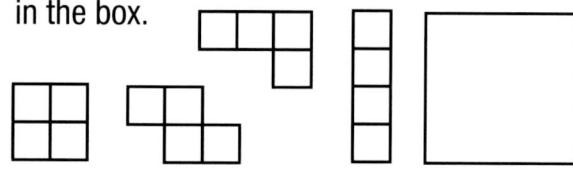

15. Circle the shape which has a vertical line (axis) of symmetry.
    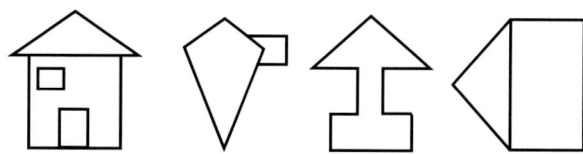

16. Roy's father is less than 100 years old. If his age is divided by 2, 3, 4, 5 or 6 there is a remainder of one. His age is:
    (a) 25   (b) 81   (c) 61   (d) 72

17. ☐ The perimeter of this rectangle is: (a) 80 mm (b) 65 mm
    (c) 75 mm (d) 70 mm

18. Complete the missing numbers in the table.

Their sum	Their product	Numbers used
13	30	10 and 3
11	28	____ and ____
9	20	____ and ____

19. Shade in the hexagon from the polygons below.
    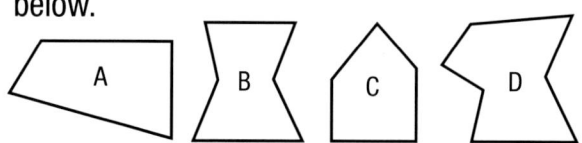

20. Put in the missing numerals in this subtraction sum.
    ```
         9 3 4 5
    −      2 _ 7 _
         _ 4 _ 7
    ```

Set 20

1. Kilo is a Greek prefix meaning:
   (a) 10   (b) 100   (c) 1000   (d) 10 000

2. How many 500-metre lengths in 2 km? _____

3. 2 kg 175 g is the same as:
   (a) 21.75 kg   (b) 2175 g
   (c) 217.5 kg   (d) 2175 kg

4. How many months do not have 31 days? _____

5. 3 hours 20 minutes is:
   (a) 320 mins   (b) 94 mins
   (c) 200 mins   (d) 302 mins

6. Use = > or < to make this statement true.

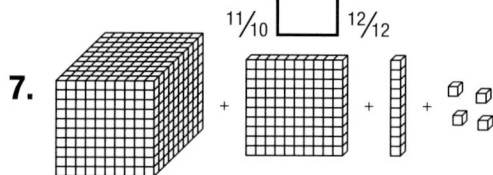

7.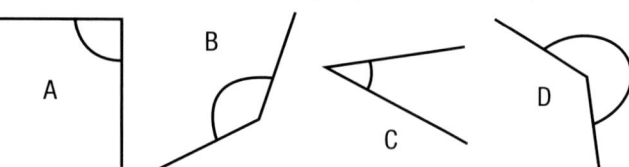

   Which number is shown in this diagram? _____

8. Circle the acute angle (less than 90°) below.

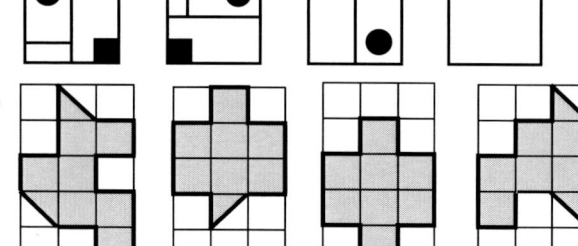

9. This pattern turns through 90° each time. Complete the last square.

10.

   A   B   C   D
   Which 2 shaded shapes above have the same area of square units?
   Shapes ☐ and ☐.

11. Circle the container which would hold one litre of water: (a) eggcup (b) bucket (c) bottle (d) spoon

12. Use the patterns to work out the missing numbers.

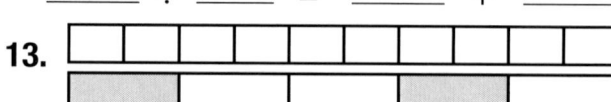

   ___ ÷ ___ = ___ + ___

13.

   The ⅖ shaded is the same as ___ -tenths.

14. The perimeter of shape ___ is 1 cm longer than the perimeter of shape ___ (ruler needed).

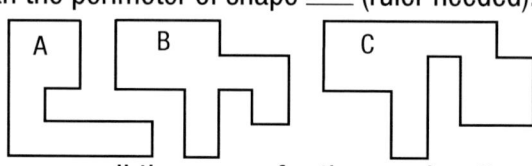

15. These are all the arrays for the number 6. Draw the arrays for the number 4 in the box.

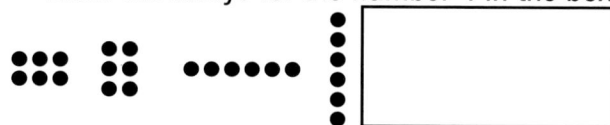

16. Write the prime numbers less than 12 in the boxes.

17. November

S	M	T	W	T	F	S
		1	2	3	4	5
6	7	8	9	10	11	12
13	14	15	16	17	18	19
20	21	22	23	24	25	26
27	28	29	30			

Circle the date which is 3 weeks after 2 November.

18. What is the total length of the vertical lines in this diagram?

   _____ cm

19. Mark catches a ball 10 times out of 10 throws. The ball is to be thrown to him an 11th time. We can predict:
   (a) he will catch it   (b) he won't catch it
   (c) he might catch it   (d) the ball will burst

20. The next shape in this series is an:
   (a) octagon   (b) square
   (c) hexagon   (d) rectangle

Set 21

1. The total value of the underlined digit in 2̲6 315 is:
   (a) 200   (b) 2000   (c) 20 000   (d) 200 000

2. To measure the height of your handwriting you would use:
   (a) metres   (b) mm   (c) cm   (d) decimetres

3. The Latin prefix 'milli' means:
   (a) ¹⁄₁₀₀ part   (b) ¹⁄₁₀ part
   (c) ¹⁄₁₀₀₀ part   (d) One millionth part

4. Five single digit numbers total 30 when added. If 4 of them are the same, what is the fifth?

5. If I assembled these faces I could make a:
   (a) cube   (b) triangular prism
   (c) cuboid   (d) cylinder

6. Put a circle round the dot that represents 175 on the number line.

7. Colour in the third circle after the fourth from the left.

8. Use the number patterns to complete the bottom row of numbers.

9. On this bar graph girl ___ is 75 cm taller than girl ___ .

10. 0.5 kg is the same as:
    (a) 1000 g   (b) 200 g   (c) 250 g   (d) 500 g

11. The sum of two numbers is 20 and their difference is 4.
    The numbers are ☐ and ☐ .

12. 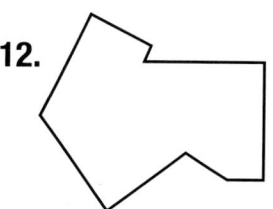 Use any method you like to find out how many right angles are inside this shape.
    ___ right angles.

13. If you use your ruler to measure paths you will find that points (intersections) ___ and ___ in this network are 3 cm apart.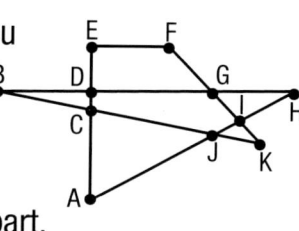

14. Circle the number which is different from the others:
    864, 375, 648, 624, 826

15. How many 25-cm pieces of string can I cut from a ball of string 2 metres long?
    ___ pieces.

16. Circle the numbers which are greater than 1200.
    1109, 1203, 1199, 1312, 1192

17. Shade in the regular polygon from the shapes below.

18. Diagram 'A' has 3 inside regions and 2 intersections (where perimeters cross).
    Diagram 'B' has ___ inside regions and ___ intersections.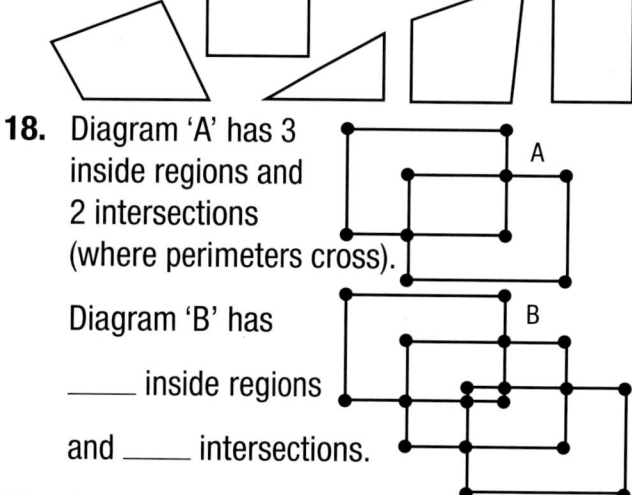

19. 14 x 3 > 21 x 2. True or false?

20. A shape with 2 parallel sides, 2 angles > 90° and 2 angles < 90° is a:
    (a) rectangle   (b) pentagon
    (c) trapezium   (d) cylinder

Set 22

1. ⅕ x 3 > ⅕ + ⅕ + ⅕. True or false?

2. Prime Number ☐ + Prime Number ☐ = Composite Number ☐

3. 50% + 0.5 + ⁵⁄₁₀ = _____

4. This prism (a polyhedron) is: 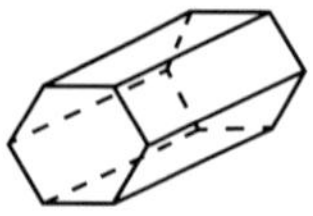
   (a) pentagonal (b) triangular
   (c) hexagonal   (d) rectangular

5. In the box draw 4 lines, each 3 cm long and all intersecting at one point.

6. Complete the letter/number series:

   A12, C10, E8, G6, _____

7. 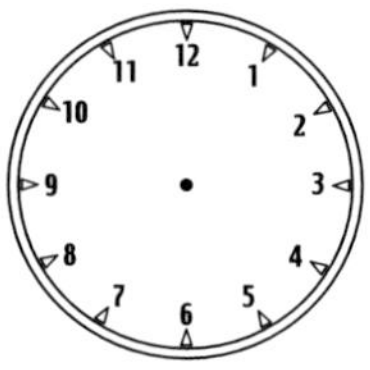  The angle between the hands of a clock at 1500 hours is:
   (a) 45°   (b) 90°
   (c) 20°   (d) 100°

8. The angles of any four-sided shape (a quadrilateral) total 360° when added.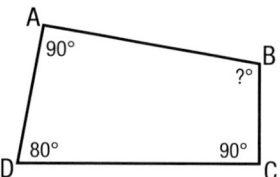

   Angle ABC = _____

9. The fraction ⅓ means:
   (a) one x three
   (b) one part out of three parts
   (c) 3 parts + 1 part
   (d) one part out of three equal parts

10. Put the numbers 6, 9, 12, 8, 16, 20 into the Venn diagram. You will have one number in the intersecting set.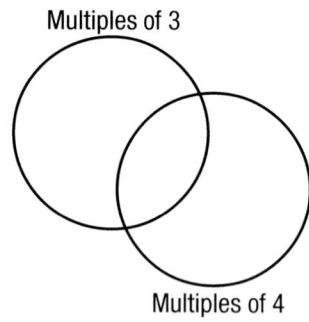

11. Write in the boxes the numbers < 20 which have both 3 and 2 as factors. ☐☐☐

12. Find the total length of the vertical line segments (ruler needed). _____ cm
    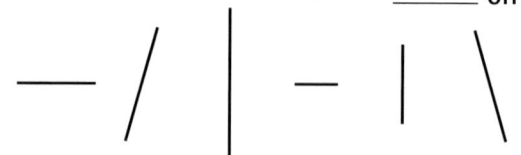

13. 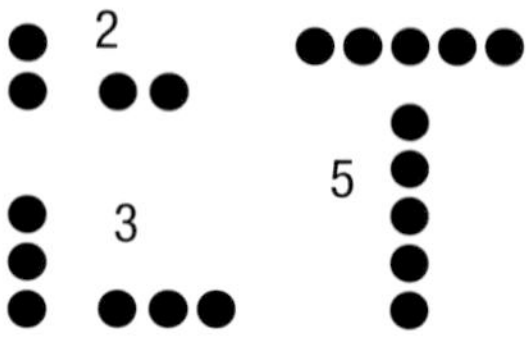 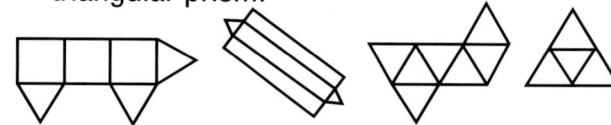 These numbers only have 2 arrays each because they are _____ numbers.

14. Circle the 'net' (a shape's flat pattern) for a triangular prism.
    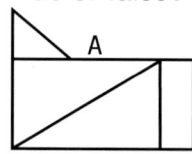 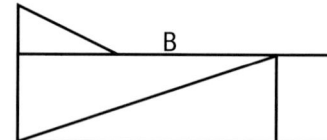

15. I am a 3-digit number. My first digit is a square number. My last digit is 3 x my second digit, which is half my first digit.

    I am: ☐☐☐

16. How many minutes from 1950 hours to 8:15 p.m.? _____ mins

17. Shapes 'A' and 'B' are similar shapes. True or false?
    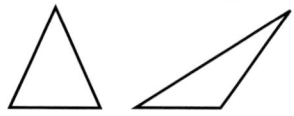 

18. Write thirteen thousand and six in figures. _____

19. Colour in the right-angled triangle.

20. Draw a triangle inside the circle so the base of the ▲ is a diameter of the circle.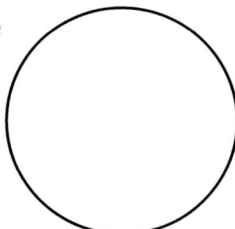

Set 23

1. ☐ < 2 x ½. Put a number in the box to make the maths sentence true.

2. Draw a shape which has 3 inside regions in the box.

3. Follow the pattern to complete the last line.
   3 x 7 = 20 + 1 + 0
   3 x 8 = 20 + 3 + 1
   3 x 9 = 20 + 5 + 2
   3 x 10 = 20 + 7 + 3
   __ x __ = __ + __ + __

4. In the box draw a four-sided shape (quadrilateral) with no lines (axes) of symmetry.

5. Circle the two multiples of 3.
   5, 10, 12, 13, 15, 17, 20

6. Which fraction is ten times bigger than ¹⁄₁₀₀?
   (a) ¹⁄₁₀   (b) ¹⁄₁₀₀₀   (c) ¹⁰⁄₁₀   (d) ½

7. In the box draw 2 triangles which intersect at 2 points.

8. 2 3 7 5 6
   Put in the decimal point in the number above so the 5 has a total value of ⁵⁄₁₀₀.

9. Shade in the right-hand box to make the shaded fractions equivalent fractions.
   ☐ is equivalent to ☐

10. The length of rectangle ☐ is twice its width (ruler needed).
    A   B   C   D

11. The distance round a netball court would be measured in:
    (a) km   (b) metres   (c) cm   (d) mm

12. Circle the digital clock which shows a time in the morning.

13. Write 3 consecutive composite numbers between 1 and 15 in the boxes.

14. If this shape was rotated clockwise through 180° (90° + 90°), draw the new shape on the cross.
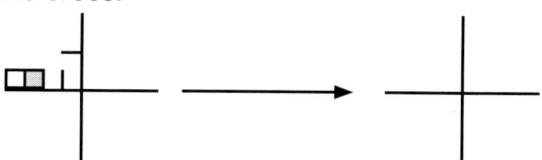

15. ≠ < > =
    Use one of these symbols to make the maths sentence true:
    5 x ⅕ ☐ 8 x ⅛

16. The area of this square is 100 mm². Its perimeter is _____ mm.

17. I have ten marbles, Tom has twice as many, and Jane has 3 x as many as Tom.
    The total number of marbles = _____.

18. The number shown on the abacus is: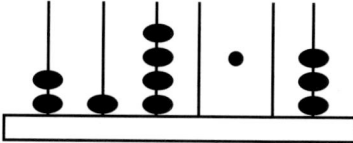
    (a) 2410.3   (b) 2140.3
    (c) 2140.03   (d) 214.03

19. Shade in the shape which is an irregular polygon.
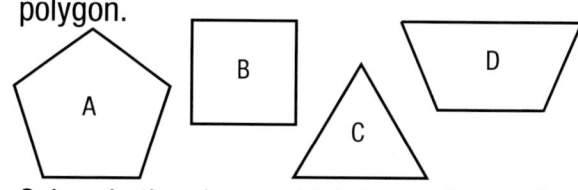

20. Colour in the shape which has only one line (axis) of symmetry.
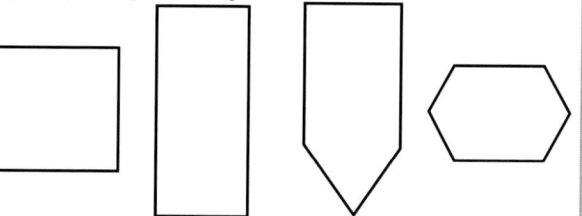

Set 24

1. 10 × ☐ = 1

2. The perimeter of this irregular pentagon is > 10 cm. True or false (ruler needed)?

3. 2.023 + 0.04 = _____

4. Circle the numbers which lie between 500 and 1500.

    1049, 1506, 1498, 499, 1502

5. Draw the diagonals in this trapezium and measure their total length. _____ cm

6. Which number between 30 and 40 is twice the product of its 2 digits? _____

7. If I cut along the diagonal of this square, what would be the total perimeter of the 2 triangles (ruler needed)? _____

8. 0.48 − 0.3 = _____

9. You would measure how much water a bucket holds in:
    (a) ml   (b) litres   (c) kilolitres   (d) grams

10. Follow the patterns and complete the last 2 lines.

    | 8 | + | 4 | = | 6 | + | 6 |
    | 10 | + | 4 | = | 7 | + | 7 |
    | 12 | + | 4 | = | 8 | + | 8 |
    | 14 | + | 4 | = | 9 | + | 9 |
    | __ | + | __ | = | __ | + | __ |
    | __ | + | __ | = | __ | + | __ |

11. What is the sum of the first 5 prime numbers?

    | 1 | 2 | 3 | 4 | 5 | 6 | 7 | 8 | 9 | 10 | 11 | 12 |

    sum = _____

12. Put in the dimensions (length and width) of this rectangle.
    _____ metres
    Perimeter = 22 m
    Area = 24 m^2
    _____ metres

13.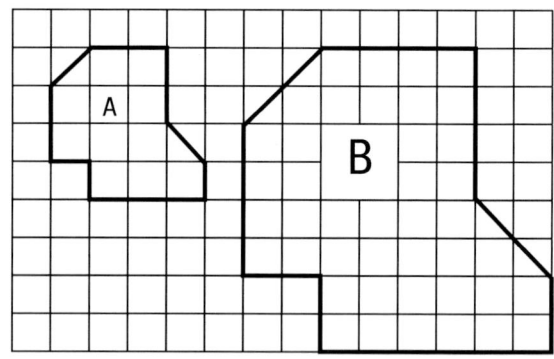
    The perimeter of shape 'B' is approximately:
    (a) 4 × shape 'A'   (b) double shape 'A'
    (c) 3 × shape 'A'   (d) 6 × shape 'A'

14. The area of the shaded face of this cube is 16 cm^2. What is the area of the whole surface of the cube? _____ cm^2

15. There are _____ pieces of wood, each 5 cm long in a metre stick.

16. 5 × 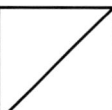 = 2.5

17. Draw in any lines (axes) of symmetry in this irregular hexagon.

18. Colour in the 2 similar shapes below.
    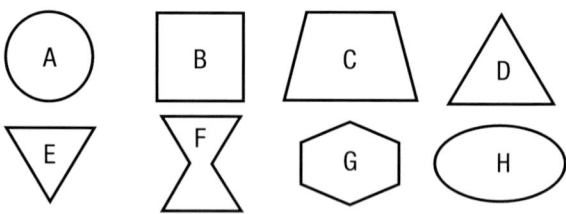

19. How many 15p pencils could I buy for £1.05?

    _____ pencils

20. Draw a triangle, labelled A B C, and show a perpendicular in the triangle labelled AX.

Set 1 – Revision

1. Six tens + 45 = _____

2. To the nearest centimetre which line below is 5 cm long? _____

   A _____
   B _____
   C _____
   D _____

3. Write the smallest number you can make with the figures 4 1 7 3: _____

4. Shade the fraction ⅛ in one of these diagrams:

   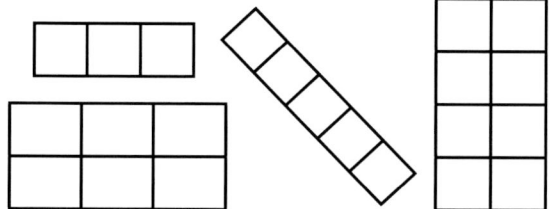

5. Complete the last basic number fact in the set below:

   7 x 5 = 35   35 ÷ 5 = 7
   5 x 7 = 35   ☐ ÷ ☐ = ☐

6. Write in figures seven thousand and two.

   _____

7. How many cubes would you stack on this grid to make a larger cube? _____

8. Think about the ½ and use your calculator to work out this sum:

   (½ of 158) + 21 = _____

9. Circle the latest time shown on the digital clocks.

10. Complete the last 2 shapes in the pattern.

11. The shaded part of this shape is:

    (a) ⅕
    (b) ¼
    (c) a fraction of the whole
    (d) ⅒

12. An ant walked _____ cm from A to B on this network of paths.

    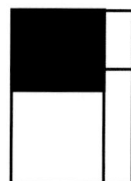

13. Use the number patterns to complete the last line:

    5 x 4 = 18 + 2
    5 x 5 = 21 + 4
    5 x 6 = 24 + 6
    5 x 7 = 27 + 8
    ☐ x ☐ = ☐ + ☐

14.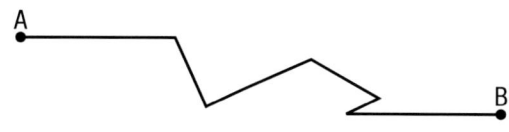

    There are _____ inside regions in this shape.

15. Fill in the missing numbers in this clockwise pattern.

    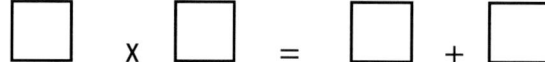
    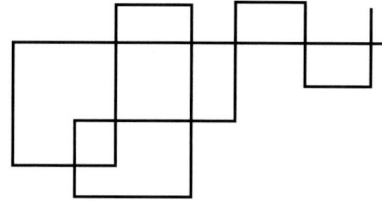

Set 2 – Revision

1. ☐ ÷ 3 = 8

2. I estimate the height of the teacher's desk is _____ cm.

3. 73 rounded to the nearest ten is _____.

4. Pens are 24p each. If I buy a pack of three for 60p I save myself _____ pence.

5. 6 x ☐ = 4 x 12

6. When zero is multiplied by any number the answer is:
   (a) always one
   (b) more than one
   (c) zero
   (d) same as the number.

7. This shape is divided into:
   (a) thirds
   (b) triangles
   (c) three parts
   (d) quarters.
   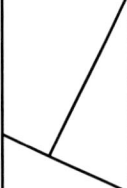

8. XV – X = _____

9.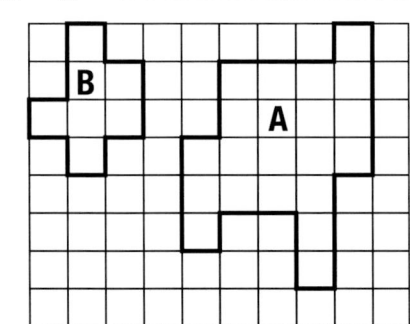

   The area of shape A is:
   (a) 2   (b) 3   (c) 4   (d) 5
   x shape B's area.

10. This diagram shows that the fraction ½ is the same as the fraction _____ .

    HALVES
    TENTHS

11.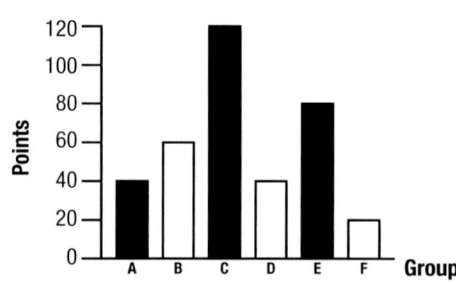

    Group _____ has 3 times as many points as group _____ but only half of group _____'s points on this block graph.

12.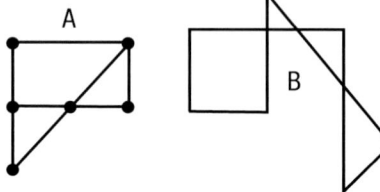

    There are 6 intersections in diagram A and _____ intersections in diagram B.

13. These are 2 of the arrays for the number 4. Draw the 3 arrays for 9 in the box.

    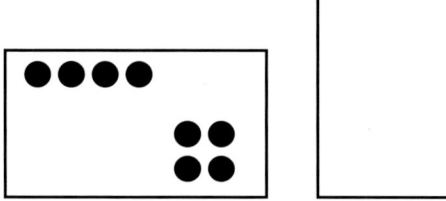 

14. This cuboid has _____ vertices (corners).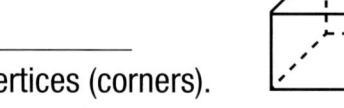

15. The diameter of a circle is twice its radius. The radius of this circle is _____ mm.

    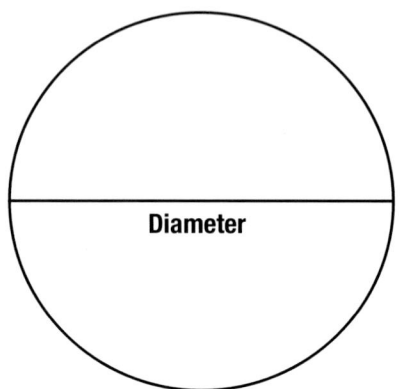
    Diameter

Set 3 – Revision

1. Shade in the odd multiples of 5.

   | 5 | 8 | 10 | 12 | 15 | 20 | 25 | 28 |

2. If you double an odd number the answer is:
   (a) always odd
   (b) odd or even
   (c) not odd or even
   (d) always even.

3. Put a cross in grid square (E,4) and shade grid square (B,2).

4. 80 x 10 = 800
   40 x 20 = 800
   20 x 40 = 800
   ☐ x ☐ = ☐

5. Dad is _____ cm tall.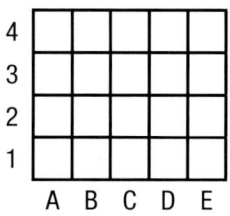

6. Complete the next domino in this pattern.
   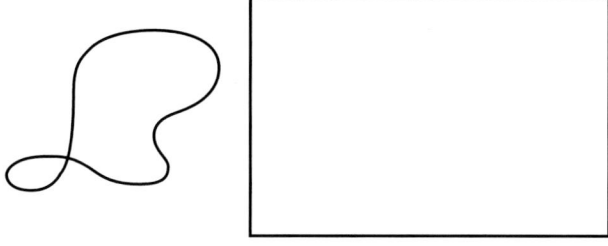

7. This is a closed curve with one intersection. Draw a closed curve with 3 intersections in the box below.

8. ●○●●○●●●●○
   _____ out of _____ circles are shaded which means 7/10 are shaded.

9. A _____
   B
   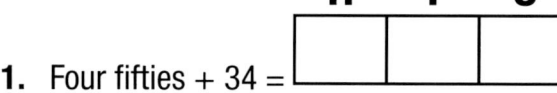

   Draw a line B that is 3 times longer than A and divide the new line into 2 equal lengths.

10. I throw two dice and a 5 and a 3 come up. My next throw will be:
    (a) a 5 and 3   (b) two 5's
    (c) two 3's   (d) I can't tell.

11. Four fifties + 34 =
    | H | T | U |
    | | | |

12. △ x ☐ x △ = 20
    The missing numbers are all prime numbers.

13. Use the addition pattern to complete the missing numbers.

16	2		12
6			
8			4

14. Draw a vertical line and a horizontal line inside this hexagon to form 2 right-angled triangles and 2 quadrilaterals.
    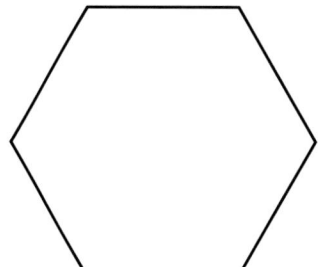

15. Concentric circles have the same centre. The width of the third largest concentric circle shown is _____ mm.
    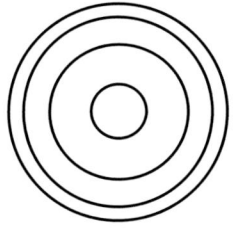

Set 4 – Revision

1. The answer to an odd number x an odd number:
   (a) is always even
   (b) is odd or even
   (c) always ends in 3
   (d) is always odd

2.

   The best number sentence for this diagram is:
   (a) 12 − 3 = 9   (b) 5 + 4 = 9
   (c) 3 x 3 = 9   (d) 8 + 1 = 9

3. Complete the next 2 numbers in the pattern:

   | 3 | 25 | 6 | 20 | 9 | 15 | □ | ___ |

4. When Peter gave me half his marbles he had 18 left. How many did he have originally?

   _____ marbles.

5.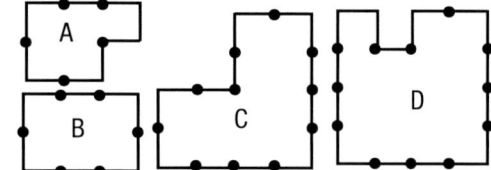

   Join the dots to form squares. The area of shape ___ is 3 x the area of shape ___ .

6. Complete the last line by following the pattern.

   43p x 100 = £43.00
   37p x 100 = £37.00
   26p x 100 = £26.00
   58p x 100 = £_____

7. Draw the pattern in box B after box A has had a ¼ turn clockwise.

8. 4 + 4 + 4 gives the same answer as:
   (a) (4 + 4) x 4   (b) 4 x 4 x 4
   (c) (4 x 2) + (4 x 1)   (d) (4 x 1) + 4

9. Show 1400 hours on the clock. The hour hand is shorter.

   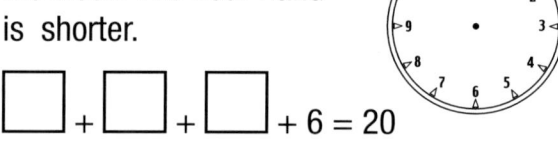

10. □ + □ + □ + 6 = 20

    The missing numbers are all different even numbers.

11. Think about the ½ and use your calculator to work out this sum:

    48 x ½ x 25 = _____

12. This pentagonal prism has ___ edges.

13. Draw 2 lines to divide this shape into 4 congruent (equal) squares. You will need to measure with your ruler.

14. Shade in the balloon which contains a number that can be divided exactly by 3, 4 and 9.

15. This line graph of Amy's test results shows that her highest mark was ___ and her lowest was ___ .

    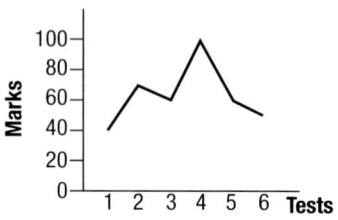

Set 5 – Revision

1. The answer to 326 x 3 is:
   (a) 946 (b) 924
   (c) 978 (d) 942

2. Use the patterns to complete the last line:
   (5 x 5) + 2 = 20 + 7
   (5 x 5) + 4 = 21 + 8
   (5 x 5) + 6 = 22 + 9
   (5 x 5) + 8 = 23 + 10
   (☐ x ☐) + ☐ = ☐ + ☐

3. 6 x ☐ x ☐ = 0

4. Draw the 4 possible arrays for the number 10 in the box.

5. A _____
   B _____
   C ____
   D _____
   Line ☐ is 2 cm longer than line ☐ but 1 cm less than line ☐.

6. Circle the numbers which can be divided into 3 equal numbers:
   16 15 20 21 23 42 99

7. 5 m 68 cm = 5.68 m
    3 m 8 cm = 3.08 m
    7 m 15 cm = 7.15 m
   so 6 m 23 cm = _____ m
      2 m 7 cm = _____ m

8. How many times bigger is the underlined 5 than the other 5 in the number 3<u>5</u>56?
   (a) 5 times (b) 50 times
   (c) 10 times (d) 100 times

9. Complete the next arrow diagram:
   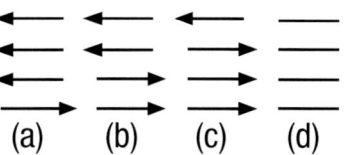
   (a) (b) (c) (d)

10. Write the 4th letter after D, the 15th letter and the 7th letter from the end of the alphabet to form the word:
    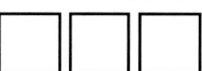

11.

12. VII x 1000 + 100 + V = ?
    Use your calculator to do this sum. Then turn the calculator upside down and write the word in the display window.

13. Move the dot 2 squares south east, then
    3 squares north,
    2 squares east,
    4 squares south west.
    Show the dot's new square.
    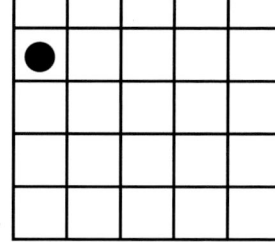

14. The number of small cubes in this diagram = _____.
    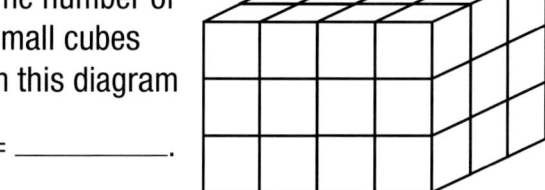

15. The area of shape A equals
    _____ squares. (Don't forget to count ½ squares too!).
    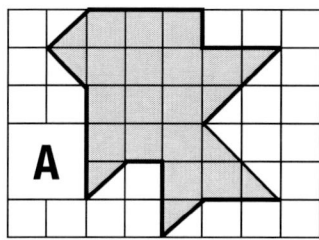

Set 6 – Revision

1. Five thousands + 12 = _____.

2. Square numbers are:
   (a) always odd   (b) odd or even
   (c) always even (d) not odd or even

3. Shade in the notes and coins needed to buy a toy for £11.35.

   | £10 | 5p | 20p | £5 | 50p | £2 | 10p | £1 |

4. Complete the next square in this rotating pattern:

   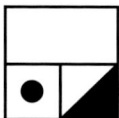  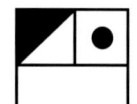 

5. The base of this pyramid is a triangle, so it has _____ vertices (corners).

6. Circle the smallest number:
   2138   2813   2381
   2318   2831   2183

7. Round 326 and 184 to the nearest hundred and find the sum of your 2 answers: _____

8.

   The third tallest flower is _____ mm high.

9. Complete the next 3 counting numbers:
   1098, 1099, _____ , _____ , _____

10. A circle's radius is half its diameter. This circle's diameter is _____ mm (use a ruler).

11. ½ kg + _____ g + _____ g = 1kg

12.

    The perimeter of shape A on this ½-cm grid is _____ cm.

13. On this block graph group A collected twice as many cans as group _____ , but only half as many as group _____ .

14. Shade in the 2 circles which total (add up to) XXV.

    (IX) (XXI) (XII) (XVI) (VII) (XIV) (XV)

15. _____ small cubes have to be added to this shape to make a 3-cm cube (i.e. a cube with all sides 3 cm long).

    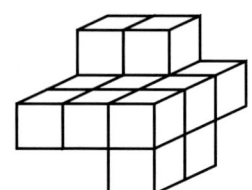

Set 7 – Revision

1.
	TT	T	H	T	U
37 x 10 =			3	7	0
37 x 100 =		3	7	0	0
37 x 1000 =					

2. 4 x 8 = 2 x 16
   20 x 4 = 10 x 8
   18 x 3 = 9 x 6
   22 x 6 = ☐ x ☐

   Use the doubling and halving pattern to fill in the missing spaces.

3. Circle the numbers which will be odd numbers when they are doubled:

   4   7   2½   6
   5   1½   3   3½

4. My pencil would weigh about:
   (a) 2 kg   (b) 10 g
   (c) 10 kg   (d) 100 g

5. TEA (6 (13) 8) COFFEE

   This Venn diagram shows that 21 adults like coffee. How many like tea? _____

6. 1 m 20 cm + 70 cm + 60 cm
   = _____ m

7. Shade in the shape which is different from the others.

   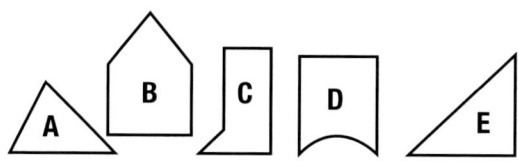

8. 6   2   4   5

   Shade in the triangular number in the above shapes.

9. £3 is made up of:
   five 20p coins + two 50p coins +
   six 10p coins + _____ 5p coins.

10. To find the perimeter of shape A I would use:
    (a) a ruler and cotton
    (b) a compass
    (c) a guess
    (d) a trundle wheel
    (e) a ruler

11. Complete the last shape of the rotating pattern below.

    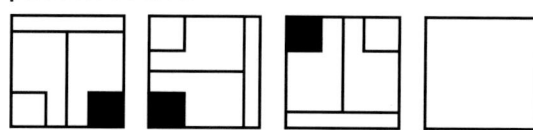

12. Use your ruler to measure and then shade in the 2 polygons with the same perimeter.

    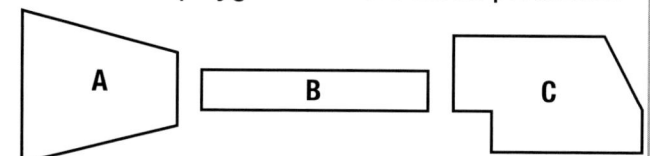

13. What is the total number of Mondays and Fridays in this month?

    August
S	M	T	W	T	F	S
		1	2	3	4	5	6
7	8	9	10	11	12	13
14	15	16	17	18	19	20
21	22	23	24	25	26	27
28	29	30	31			

    _____

14. Use your calculator to find how many lots of 24 there are in 6000. _____ lots.

15. Shade in 3 semi-circles, one to the left of the centre circle and two to the right.

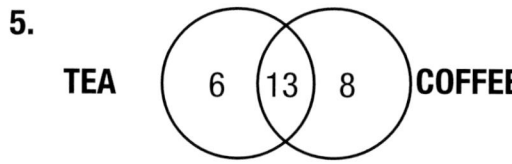

Set 8 – Revision

1. XIX + IV + VII = ☐   Answer in Roman Numerals.

2. Join some dots to make 2 right-angled triangles.

3. The answer to the sum 2 x 6 x 4 x 2 is ODD | EVEN (shade your answer).

4. Complete the next 2 numbers in the series:

   AA4 AB6 AC8 AD10 _____ _____

5. Shade the 2 solid shapes with the same number of faces:

   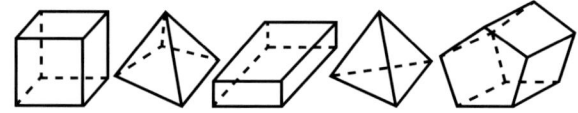

6. On this ½-cm grid draw a shape which has a perimeter of 7 cm.

7. Circle the even numbers:

   8   1033   2768   2911   3020   77   1084

8. The fraction shaded is:
   (a) ¾
   (b) ½
   (c) ⅝
   (d) 4/4

9.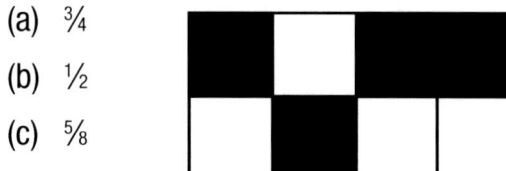

   Ian   Roy   Bob   Ann

   _____ and _____ are both taller than _____ but shorter than _____.

10. Eight hundreds – four fifties = two fifties + _____.

11. If an even number can be exactly divided by 4 it can also be exactly divided by:

    (a) 8   (b) 3   (c) 2   (d) 12

12. The numbers 2, 3 and 4 will all divide into 24 exactly so it is shaded. Shade other numbers which have the same 3 factors.

24	28	20
30	36	16
40	12	60

13. This shape has one outside region and _____ inside regions.

    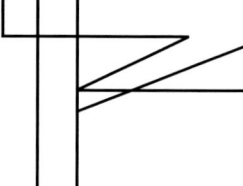

14. A _____
    B _____
    C _____
    D _____
    E _____
    F _____

    I could use lines ☐, ☐, ☐ and ☐ to make a rectangle (use a ruler).

15. Share £20 among three girls so that Amy has four times as much as Ann who has £2 less than Toni.

    Amy £_____
    Ann £_____
    Toni £_____

Set 9 – Revision

1.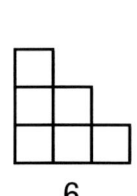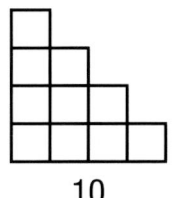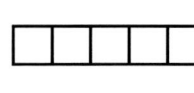
   3   6   10   ____
   Complete the pattern of triangular numbers above.

2. If you rearrange the digits of 274 you can make the numbers:
   247, 724, 472, 427 and ☐.
   Circle the smallest number.

3. 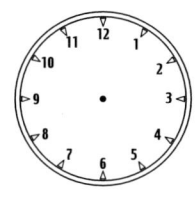 Draw the hands on the clock to show 10.40 p.m.

4. 4 + 70 + 500 = ☐☐☐ (H T U)

5. The product of 6 and 4 is the same as the product of:
   (a) 7 and 5   (b) 3 and 9
   (c) 3 and 8   (d) 5 and 6

6. _____
   I estimate the length of this line to be about:
   (a) 15 cm   (b) 9 cm
   (c) 25 cm   (d) 6 cm

7.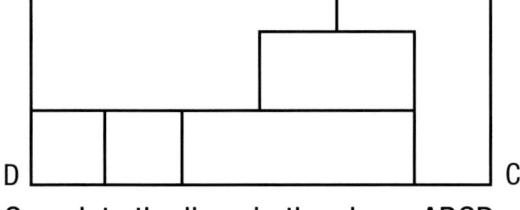
   Complete the lines in the shape ABCD above to divide it into squares.
   Its area is ____ squares (cm²).

8. Half of line A below is ____ cm or ____ mm (use a ruler).
   A _____

9. John and Sue shared 24 marbles between them so that Sue had twice as many as John.
   John had ____ marbles.
   Sue had ____ marbles.

10. (6 x 4) = 20 + 4
    (6 x 5) = 24 + 6
    (6 x 6) = 28 + 8
    (6 x 7) = 32 + 10
    (☐ x ☐) = ☐ + ☐

11. ☐ + ☐ = ☐ + ☐
    The missing numbers are the first 4 digits.

12. If you double the length of each side of shape A the new shape has ____ times as many squares in its area.

13. The numbers in the boxes are all multiples of 3. Write in the missing multiple of 3 which is less than 30.

3	15	24
27		9
12	18	6

14. The total length of all edges on this triangular prism = ____ cm (use a ruler).

15.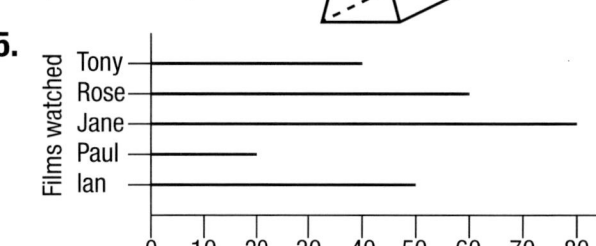
    Tony, Rose, Jane, Paul, Ian — Films watched
    0 10 20 30 40 50 60 70 80
    This bar graph shows that ☐ has seen 3 times as many films as ☐.

Set 10 – Revision

1. 20 × 3 [>] [<] [=] 5 × 11

2. 100 ml × [   ] = 1 litre

3. Shade in the shape which has no right angles.

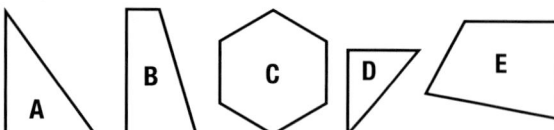

4. An odd number + two even numbers always give an [ODD] [EVEN] number. Shade your answer.

5. I estimate the height of my desk to be _____ cm.

6. Circle the objects which are heavier than one kilogram:

   pencil   **C.D.**   **door**
   brick   **balloon**   **car**

7. Circle the fraction which is more than one half:

   ⁴⁄₁₀   ⅕   ⅝   ⅓   ²⁄₄

8. A rectangle's length is 10 cm. Its perimeter is 28 cm. Its measurements are:
   (a) 10 cm and 6 cm   (b) 10 cm and 5 cm
   (c) 8 cm and 10 cm   (d) 10 cm and 4 cm

9.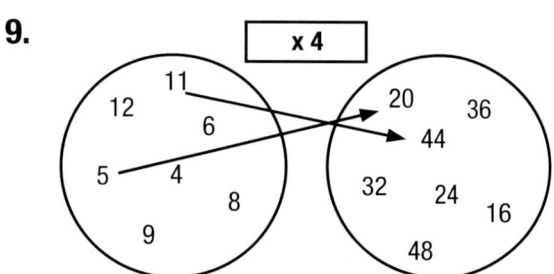

   Draw the rest of the arrows to complete this mapping diagram by using the relation sign in the box.

10. £5 + 50p + 20p =
    £2 + £1 + 50p + ◯ + 20p

11. Use the number patterns to complete the last line:

    (2 × 4) = 10 − 2
    (4 × 4) = 20 − 4
    (6 × 4) = 30 − 6
    (8 × 4) = 40 − 8
    ([ ] × [ ]) = [ ] − [ ]

12. Colour in the 4-sided shapes (quadrilaterals) in this diagram.

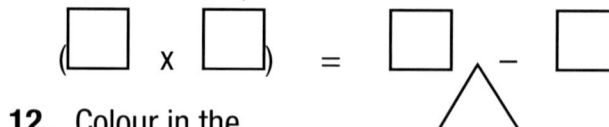

13.
	5 × table	11 × table
Odd		11
Even	10	

Use the numbers less than 35 to fit into the Carroll diagram. Two have been done for you.

14. The longest side of this 8-sided shape (octagon) is

    ____ cm or

    ____ mm longer than its shortest side.

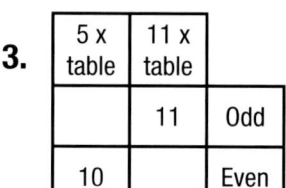

15.

    Alan   Pat   Jean   Mary

    [   ] is taller than [   ] and [   ] but shorter than [   ].

Set 11 – Revision

1. Any odd number divided by itself gives an answer which is:
   (a) odd or even (b) even
   (c) odd (d) not odd or even

2. Colour in the one semi-circle in the diagram.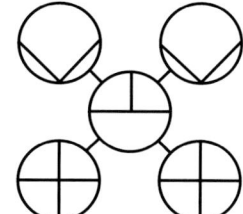

3. \> = < ÷ x
   Use one of these symbols to make this maths sentence true:
   15 + 20 ☐ 5 x 7

4.

   Circle the digital clock which shows 1 p.m.

5. Put these fractions in order from lowest to highest: ¼ ¹⁄₂₀ ½
   ___ , ___ , ___

6. If 2 even numbers are added to any odd number the answer is always:
   (a) even (b) odd or even
   (c) correct (d) odd

7. 4 cm² is about the area of:
   (a) a door (b) a book
   (c) a stamp (d) a pool

8. Circle the shape which is reflected on either side of a line drawn across its centre from left to right.
   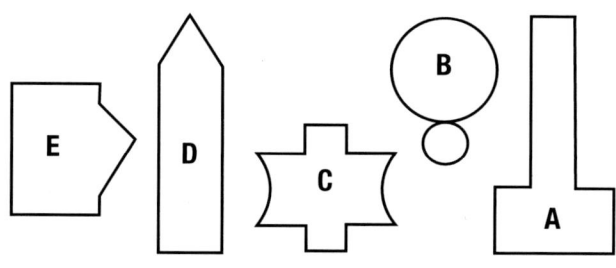

9. 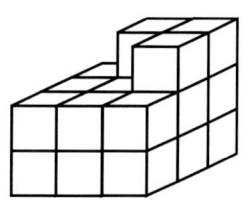 Shade in grid square (5, 3) and put a cross in grid square (2, 4).

10.  How many small cubes would I have if I doubled the number in this shape?
    _____ small cubes.

11. Share £30 among Roy, Ann and Peta so Ann gets three times as much as Roy and £5 more than Peta.
    Ann's share £_____
    Peta's share £_____
    Roy's share £_____

12. Rule 3 lines to divide this shape into 4 congruent (equal) triangles.

13. Complete this mapping diagram.
    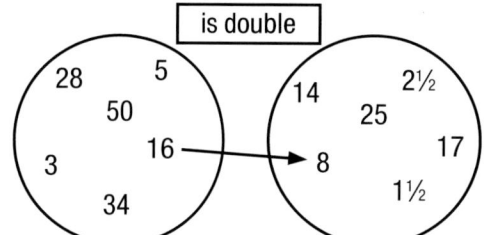

14. Shade in the number which is the product of 2 other numbers in the circle.
    36, 30, 24, 7, 9, 6, 5, 8, 32

15. Fill in this Venn diagram with numbers up to 25.
    multiples of 3 | multiples of 4
    (3, 12, 4)

Set 12 – Revision

1. 4 + 4 + 4 = ☐ + (2 x ☐)
   The missing numbers are both the same.

2.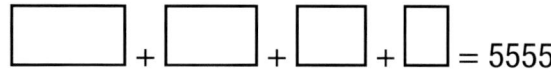
   There are ___ different kinds of shapes in this diagram.

3. If I counted from 1 to 10 with a second between each number it would take me:
   (a) 10 seconds   (b) 8 seconds
   (c) 9 seconds   (d) 11 seconds

4. Follow a pattern to find the missing numbers:
   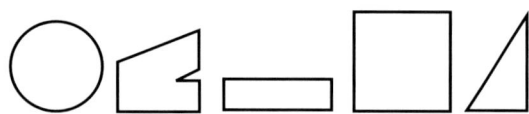 = 5555

5. Shade in the shapes which will **tessellate** (i.e. fit together without gaps between the shapes).
   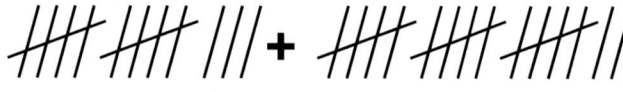

6. Rounding 2537 to the nearest ten is:
   (a) 2530   (b) 2540
   (c) 2400   (d) 2545

7. The tallies show:
   (a) 4 + 3   (b) 10 + 10
   (c) 13 + 17   (d) 13 + 13
   ╫╫ ╫╫ ||| + ╫╫ ╫╫ ╫╫ ||

8. I have £10. Roy has twice as much and Jane has half as much. How much do we have altogether? £ _____

9. 50 + 200 + 200 + 50 + 100 + 100
   How many fifties do we have if we add the above numbers?
   _____ fifties.

10. The total length of the horizontal lines in this shape is
    _____ cm or
    _____ mm.
    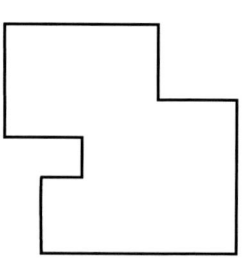

11. If I draw a straight line joining the vertices that are opposite each other, how many triangles will I form?
    (a) 6 (b) 20 (c) 18 (d) 24

12.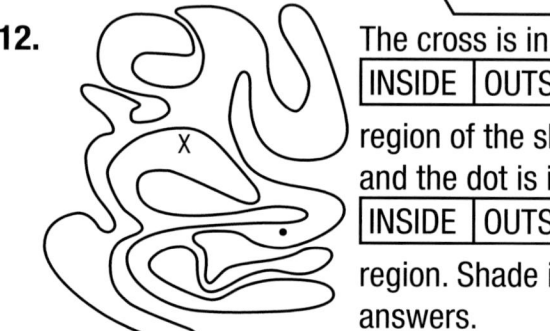
    The cross is in the INSIDE / OUTSIDE region of the shape and the dot is in the INSIDE / OUTSIDE region. Shade in your answers.

13. **December**

S	M	T	W	T	F	S
		1	2	3	4	5
6	7	8	9	10	11	12
13	14	15	16	17	18	19
20	21	22	23	24	25	26
27	28	29	30	31		

    The total number of Mondays and Thursdays in this month is _____.

14. There are no ODD / EVEN multiples of ten because 10 is an ODD / EVEN number. Shade in your answers.

15. There are 31 children in a class. 14 like art and sport. 8 like only sport. How many like only art? Use the Venn diagram below to find out.
    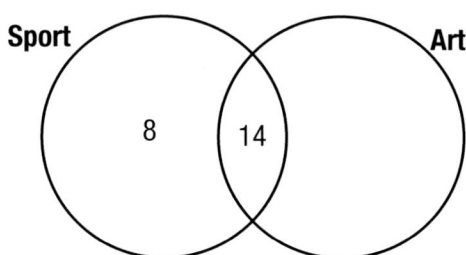

Set 13 – Revision

1. 4½ x 5 ☐ 5 x 4½
   Use the correct symbol (≠ > = <) to make the maths sentence true.

2. 9 squared (9^2) – 9 = _____

3. Complete the series:
   1.01, 1.04, 1.07, 1.10, _____

4. Write all the odd composite numbers < 30 in the boxes.
   ☐ ☐ ☐ ☐

5. 1700 metres – ½ km = _____ metres.

6. $^{11}/_{12}$ – $^{5}/_{12}$ = $^{1}/_{12}$ + ☐/₁₂

7. ☐ x ☐ x ☐ = 110
   Each missing number is a different prime.

8. Circle the 2 solid shapes (polyhedra) which have fewer than 9 edges.
   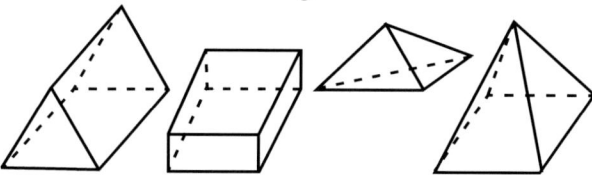

9. Round 3627 to the nearest 10: _____.

10. 8 x 43 = (8 x ☐) + (8 x 3)

11. Draw a tally for 18 in sets of 5.

12. Circle the right angle (90°)
    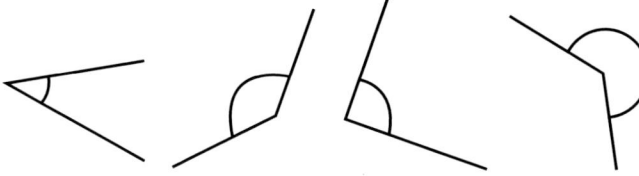

13. In 6 hours this digital clock will show _____.

14. Use the patterns to complete the columns.
    | 4 | x | 2 | = | 5 | + | 3 |
    | 4 | x | 4 | = | 10 | + | 6 |
    | 4 | x | 6 | = | 15 | + | 9 |
    | 4 | x | 8 | = | 20 | + | 12 |
    | __ | x | 10 | = | __ | + | __ |

15. With a pack of cards I turn up a king, then a three, then a four. My next card will be:
    (a) a queen   (b) a king
    (c) a five   (d) I can't predict

16. 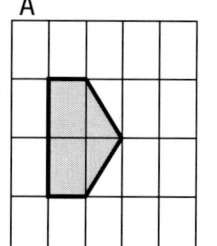 The length of the pentagon's diagonal is:
    _____ cm or _____ mm.

17. The area of any shape is:
    (a) its length x width
    (b) the number of square units it covers
    (c) the distance round it
    (d) twice its length and twice its breadth

18. Shaded area ☐ is 3 times shaded area ☐.
    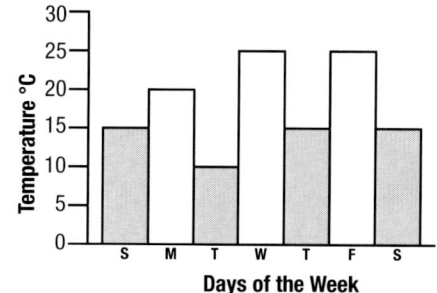
    A   B   C

19. 3.5 metres < 350 cm. True or false?

20. The temperature on ☐ was double that on ☐.

Set 14 – Revision

1. Write 4006 in words. _____

2. 3 m 21 cm to the nearest metre = ____ m.

3. $\frac{5}{10} > \frac{3}{6}$ True or false?

4. 27 = 3 x ☐ x 3

5. The number of 1-cm cubes in this solid shape = ____

6. This tally of 10-kg blocks of wood totals ____ kg.

7. A _____
   B _____
   C _____
   D _____
   Line segment ____ is 1cm longer than line segment ____.

8. Complete the last row by using the patterns.
   24 ÷ 3 = 4 + 4
   240 ÷ 3 = 40 + 40
   2 400 ÷ 3 = 400 + 400
   ____ ÷ ____ = ____ + ____

9. Round the numbers in the boxes to complete the maths sentence.
   48 x 19 ≈ ____ x ____ = 1000

10. 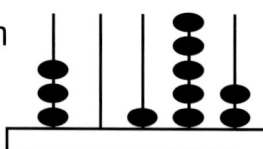 The shaded area contains ☐/10

11. The number shown on the abacus is:

12. 4 x (☐ + 5) = 24

13. A scalene triangle has no congruent sides. Use your ruler to check and shade in the scalene ▲ below.
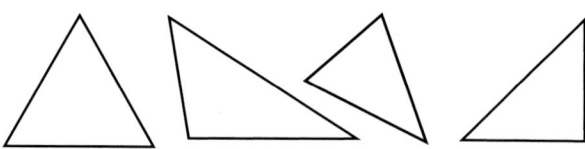

14. The arrow turns clockwise through 450° (90° + 90° + 90° + 90° + 90°). Show its new position.

15. Tickets for a school outing were £4 each. The teacher collected £96. How many pupils went? ____

16. This Venn diagram shows the results of a class survey.
    ____ liked summer.
    ____ liked both.
    ____ liked only winter.
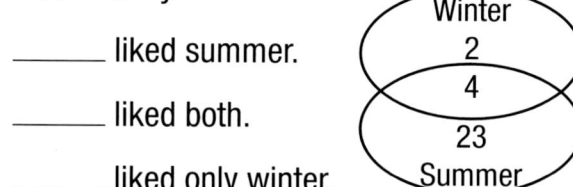

17. 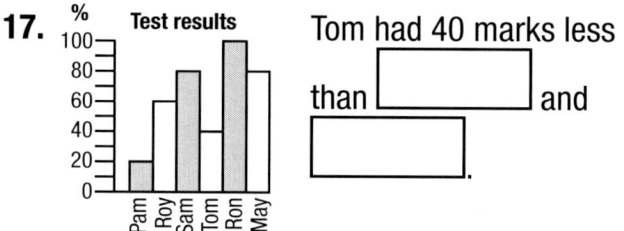 Tom had 40 marks less than ☐ and ☐.

18. 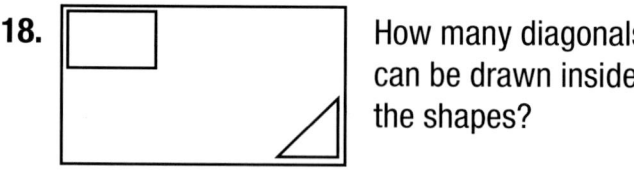 How many diagonals can be drawn inside the shapes? ____

19. Can you travel over this network of paths without going over the same path twice?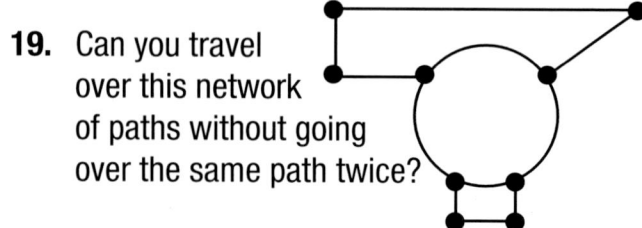
____

20. Circle the objects whose mass is measured in kilograms.

rubber   rock   coin   sock   fruit

Set 15 – Revision

1. 40 × ☐ = 1200

2. ☐5☐ × 8 / 4☐5 6 Put in the missing numbers in this algorithm (sum).

3. [dice showing 4, 5, 6, ☐] Complete the final square by following the pattern.

4. XIX + VI = 17 + ☐ Answer in Roman numerals.

5. Line 'C' is ___ cm shorter than the longest line.
   A _____
   B _____
   C ____   D _____

6. A beetle's mass would be measured in:
   (a) kilograms (b) grams (c) tonnes (d) litres

7. Colour in the 3-dimensional shapes.
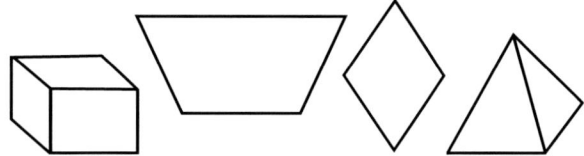

8. Take the sum of 5, 10 and 12 away from 35.

9. (3 + 9) + 4 = 3 + (9 + ☐)

10. Write the odd composite numbers between 25 and 40 in the boxes.

11. How many small cubes would you put on this grid to make a large cube? ____

12. There are 2 red jacks in a pack of 52 cards so I have a 2 in 52 (or 1 in 26) chance of drawing a red jack. What chance of drawing a king?

    (a) 1 in 52 (b) 4 in 52 (c) 4 in 26 (d) 1 in 26

13. $2^3 = 2 \times 2 \times 2 = 8$
    $4^2 = 4 \times 4 = 16$
    $1^4 = $ _____ = ☐

14. 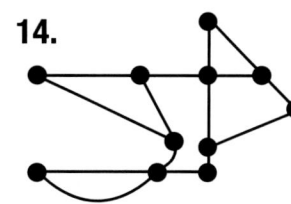 How many regions in this network of paths? Remember there is an outside region too.
    _____ regions

15. Draw in any line (axis) of symmetry you can see in this shape.
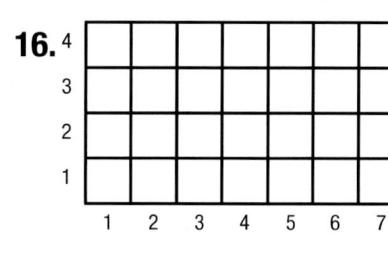

16. [grid 7×4] Shade in coordinate square (4,2) and put a cross in coordinate square (1,3).

17. [clock showing 6:00] In ½ an hour the time on this clock will be:
    (a) 1630 (b) 6:15 a.m.
    (c) 1830 (d) 12:30 p.m.

18. Circle the shapes which will not tessellate (fit together with no gaps).

19. Draw a line 60 mm long in the box and then divide it into three equal (congruent) lengths.

20. The estimated perimeter (circumference) of this circle is _____ cm.

Set 16 – Revision

1. The total value of the underlined digit in the number 362.1<u>5</u> is:
   (a) 5   (b) 5/10   (c) 5/1000   (d) 5/100

2. Write the smallest possible number with the digits: 4, 2, 7, 9, 3.

3. The common numeral for
   200 + 7 units + 3/10 is: _____

4. 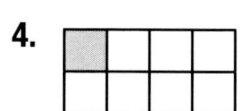 + (circle diagram)
   Total fraction shaded is:
   (a) 3/8   (b) 3/6   (c) 3/12   (d) 2/3

5. 3.09 > 3.2 True or false?

6. Look at the pattern between rows X and Y and complete the grid.

X	3	5	2	6	1
Y	9	25	4		

7. Show the number 3204 on the abacus.

8. 397 + 106 ≈ (is approximately):
   (a) 600   (b) 400   (c) 300   (d) 500

9. A ten-year-old boy could walk a kilometre in about:
   (a) 2 mins   (b) 5 mins
   (c) 15 mins   (d) 90 secs

10.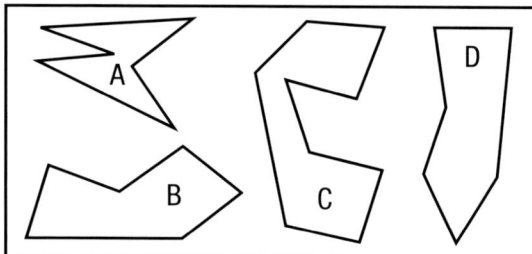
    Measure with your ruler and then shade in the shapes with the same perimeter.

11. Circle the set of numbers between 1090 and 1200 from the list below.
    1100, 1080, 1210, 1030, 1099

12. Circle the array which shows a prime number.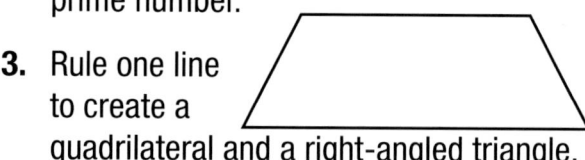

13. Rule one line to create a quadrilateral and a right-angled triangle.

14. Complete the maths sentence below:
    ☐ × 2 = 1

15. Using only the numbers 40, 8 and 5 complete the different basic number facts below:
    40 ÷ 8 = 5
    ___ ÷ ___ = ___
    ___ × ___ = ___
    ___ × ___ = ___

16. In this network the total length of paths between intersections ☐ and ☐ is 4½ cm.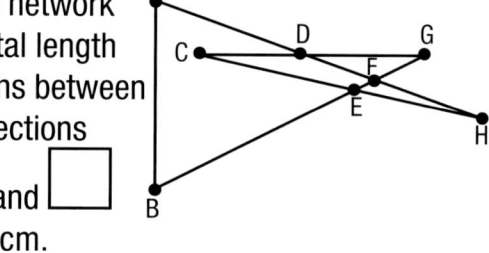

17. Roy put £6 a week into his bank account. After 10 weeks he's only drawn out £25. How much is left in his account?

18. Circle the 2 clocks which show the same time.

19. Can you draw along all the paths in this network without going over the same path twice? _____

20. Rule arrows in this mapping diagram. The pairs must agree with the relation sign in the box.

    is a multiple of
    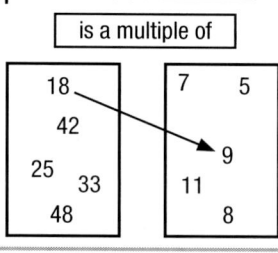

Set 17 – Revision

1. The number which is 17 less than 1000 is: _____ .

2. 5 x 0 x 6 = 6 x 5 x 0 True or false?

3. Circle the whole numbers:

    ²⁄₃   ⁸⁄₈   ¹¹⁄₁₂   ⁹⁄₁₀   ⁵⁄₅   ¹⁄₄

4. Complete the series:

    KL3, MN6, OP9, _____, _____ .

5. Points ☐ and ☐ are 3½ cm apart (ruler needed).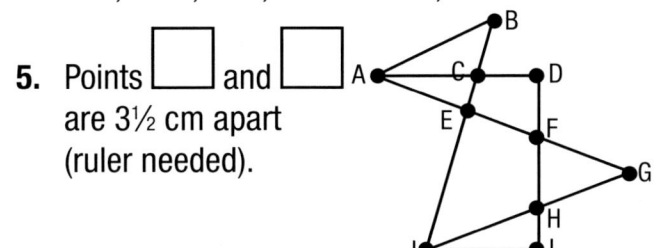

6. Put the composite numbers between 40 and 50 in the boxes:

    ☐☐☐☐☐

7. Using only the digits 3, 2, 6 write the numbers greater than 300:

    (a) _____   (b) _____

    (c) _____   (d) _____

8. We would measure the distance between towns in:
    (a) metres   (b) km   (c) mm   (d) cm

9. The time shown is:
    (a) 10.35   (b) 7.45
    (c) 9.35   (d) 9.50

10. 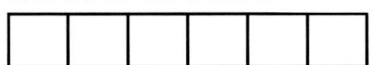 Shade in all the squares which touch a square on the perimeter of the grid.

11. Follow the rotating (turning) pattern and draw the next tetromino in the box:

    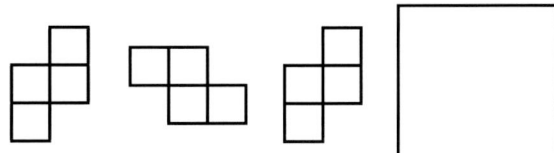

12. Complete the missing numbers on the number line. No improper fractions (e.g. ¹⁵⁄₁₂) can be used.

13. Draw a shape with no vertices in the box.

14. I double the sum of 6 and ____ and the answer is 32. Put in the missing number.

15. In which direction would you travel if you went from the dot to grid point C2?
    (a) NW   (b) SW   (c) SE   (d) NE

    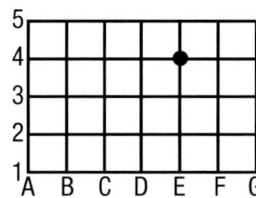

16. The missing numbers are 3 different prime numbers.

    ☐ x ☐ x ☐ = 70

17. 4 x 0 x 3 x 2 < 1 x 2 x 4 True or false?

18. Circle the shape which has one horizontal line (axis) of symmetry.

    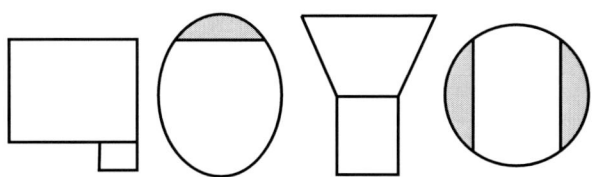

19. 3 x ¼ kg = _____ grams.

20. Circle the arrays which show triangular numbers.

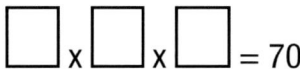

Set 18 – Revision

1. The total value of the 4 in 2435 is:
   (a) 4   (b) 400   (c) 40   (d) 4000

2. 2.63 = 2 + ☐/10 + ☐/100

3. This triangular-based pyramid is made up of:
   (a) 3 triangles
   (b) 2 triangles
   (c) 4 triangles
   (d) 3 triangles and a square

4. The lowest multiple of 2, 4 and 5 is _____.

5. Circle the two dots which are 2 cm from a vertex (corner).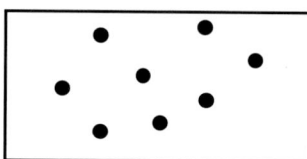

6. Look at the patterns and complete the last line:
   (10 x 1000) – 10 = 9990
   (9 x 1000) – 9 = 8991
   (8 x 1000) – 8 = 7992
   (7 x 1000) – 7 = 6993
   (6 x 1000) – 6 = 5994
   (☐ x ☐) – ☐ = ☐

7. You would measure the width of a road in:
   (a) cm   (b) metres   (c) mm   (d) km

8. Join the other vertices of this shape to point P.

9. 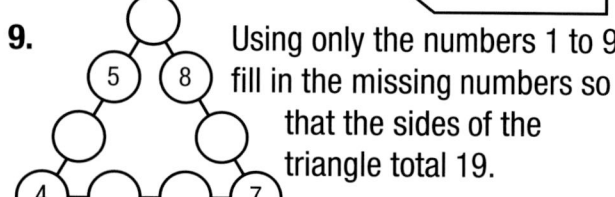 Using only the numbers 1 to 9 fill in the missing numbers so that the sides of the triangle total 19.

10. Shade in the shape which has no right angles:
    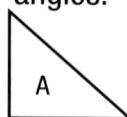 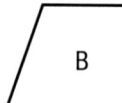 
    A B C D

11. Three books and two toys cost £31. The toys are £5 each. The books each cost the same price.

    The cost of one book = £_____

12. A _____
    B _____
    C _____
    D _____
    When added, the total length of the longest and the shortest line segment above is _____ cm.

13. 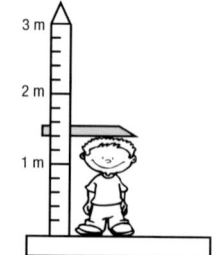 Peter is _____ cm tall.

14. IV x ☐ = XXIV

15. Town A is _____ km from town B.
    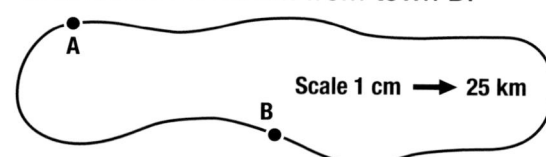
    Scale 1 cm → 25 km

16. Mary ate 4/10 of a chocolate bar. David ate 2/10. Ken ate ½ of the rest. Shade in what was left:
    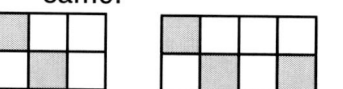

17. Circle the shaded fractions which are the same.
    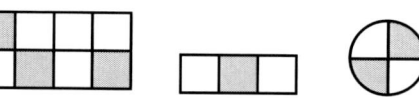

18. Circle the time which is about 4.30 p.m.

19. If you stacked 5 of these shapes on top of each other you would have a:
    (a) cube
    (b) cylinder
    (c) triangular prism
    (d) triangle

20. On this ½-cm grid the area shaded = _____ cm². (Four ½-cm squares = 1 cm²)
    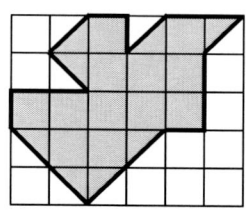

Set 19 – Revision

1. (14 × 4) – ☐ = 56

2. If the last 2 digits of these dates can be exactly divided by 4 then the date is a leap year. Circle the leap years below:

    1942, 1964, 1971, 1972, 1902

3. Write the odd multiples of 3 between 10 and 40 in the boxes.

4. The perimeter of the shaded shape on this 2-cm grid is

    _____ cm

    or _____ mm.

5. Put these decimal fractions in descending order (from largest to least): 2.8, 2.08, 2.02, 2.51, 0.88

    _____, _____, _____, _____, _____

6.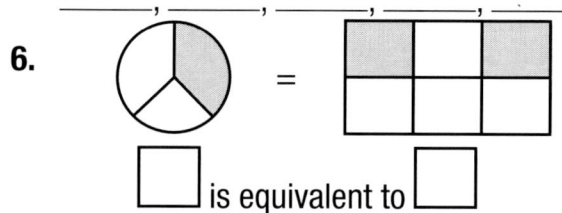

7. Circle the horizontal line segment which is 10 mm long.

8. Shade in the clock which shows 1800 hours.

9. A rounding estimate of the answer to 198 + 302 + 210 is:
    (a) 600 (b) 700 (c) 500 (d) 800

10. The place value of the underlined digit in 32.4<u>7</u> is:
    (a) units (b) tens (c) 100ths (d) 10ths

11. What is the second highest number that can be written with only 3 digits?

    _____

12. Measure and then draw lines in the rectangle to show it has an area of 8 cm².

13. I estimate the length of the teacher's desk is _____ cm.

14. This is a tromino. There is only one other and it is a different shape but uses the 3 squares. Draw it in the box.

    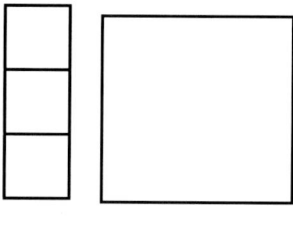

15. Circle the shape which has only one vertical line (axis) of symmetry.

16. Ken's father is less than 50 years old. If his age is divided by 2, 3, 4, 9 and 12 there is always a remainder of one.

    His age is _____ years.

17. The perimeter of shape A is 3 times longer than shape 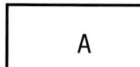's perimeter.

    | A | B | C | D |

18. Complete the 2 missing numbers in the table.

Their sum	Their product	Numbers used
15	50	10 and 5
11	24	___ and ___
7	12	3 and 4

19. Shade in the pentagon from the polygons below.

20. Put in the missing numerals in this subtraction sum:

    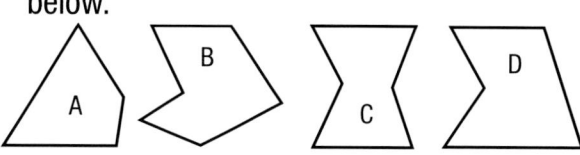

Set 20 – Revision

1. Penta is a Greek prefix meaning:
   (a) 10   (b) 5   (c) 6   (d) 100

2. How many 500-metre lengths in 1½ km?

3. 2 L 126 ml is the same as:
   (a) 21.26 litres   (b) 212.6 litres
   (c) 2126 ml   (d) 2126 litres

4. The total number of days in the last 3 months of the year = _____ days.

5. 14 weeks 3 days is:
   (a) 143 days   (b) 102 days
   (c) 101 days   (d) 341 days

6. Use =, < or > to make this statement true:
   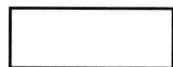
   ⅗ ☐ 9/10

7.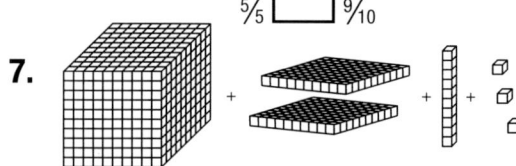
   Which number is shown in this diagram?
   _____

8. Circle the obtuse angle (between 90° and 180°) below:
   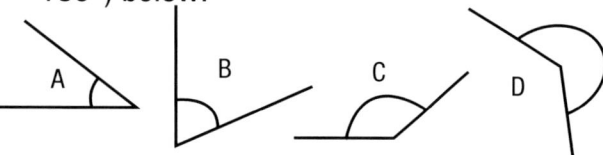

9. Use the vertical patterns to work out the missing numbers.
   3 x 6 = 18 = 0 + 18
   4 x 6 = 24 = 10 + 14
   5 x 6 = 30 = 20 + 10
   6 x 6 = 36 = 30 + 6
   ☐ x ☐ = ☐ = ☐ + ☐

10. This pattern turns through 90° each time. Complete the last square.

11. Estimate how much water a jam jar would hold.
    (a) 5 ml   (b) 5 litres   (c) 500 ml   (d) 2 litres

12. Which 2 shaded shapes below have the same area of square units?
    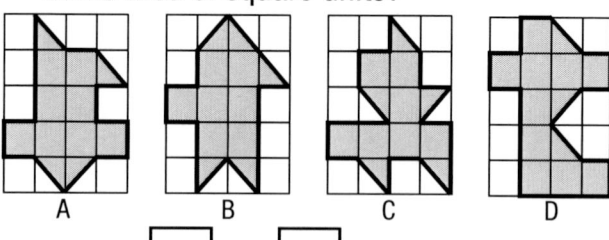
    Shapes ☐ and ☐.

13.
    The ¼ shaded is the same as _____-eighths.

14. Shapes _____ and _____ have the same perimeter (ruler needed).
    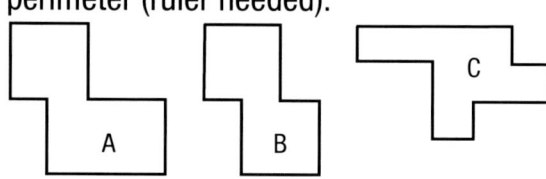

15. These are the arrays for the prime number 5. Draw the arrays for the prime number 3 in the box.
    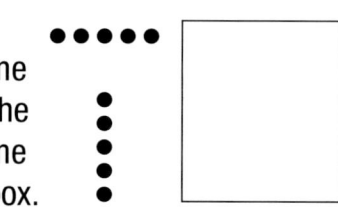

16. The only even prime number is _____.

17. March
S	M	T	W	T	F	S
			1	2	3	4
5	6	7	8	9	10	11
12	13	14	15	16	17	18
19	20	21	22	23	24	25
26	27	28	29	30	31	

    Circle the date which is 3 weeks and 2 days after 2 March.

18. What is the total length of the parallel lines in this diagram? _____ cm

19. When Sandra cut a pack of cards she turned up a king, a queen, and a king. Her next card would be:
    (a) a queen   (b) a king
    (c) we can't tell   (d) an ace

20. The next shape in this series is a:
    (a) triangle   (b) quadrilateral
    (c) pentagon   (d) circle

Set 21 – Revision

1. The total value of the underlined digit in 37 864 is:
   (a) 70 000   (b) 7   (c) 7 000   (d) 70

2. To measure the length of a bridge we would use:
   (a) cm   (b) mm   (c) m   (d) ml

3. The Greek prefix 'octa' means:
   (a) six   (b) five   (c) eight   (d) four

4. An unknown number is half the product of 3 and 16. The number is _____ .

5.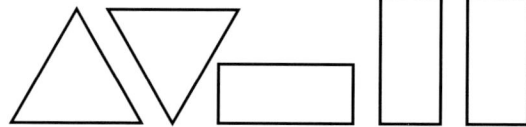
   If I assemble these faces I could make a:
   (a) pyramid   (b) cylinder
   (c) triangular prism   (d) rectangular prism

6. Put a circle around the dot that represents 1.8 on the number line.

7. Colour in the circle which is 2 places to the right of the centre circle.

8. Use the number patterns to complete the bottom row of numbers.
   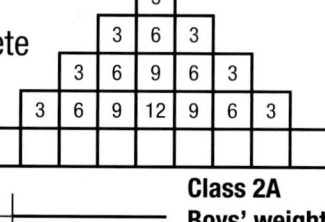

9. On this bar graph boy _____ weighs twice as much as boy _____ .
   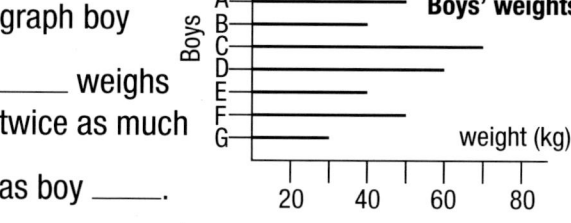

10. 1500 ml is the same as:
    (a) 150 l   (b) 15 l   (c) 1.5 l   (d) 1.25 l

11. Circle the number which is different from the others:
    15, 9, 13, 18, 21, 26

12. The sum of two numbers is 16 and their difference is 2.
    The numbers are ☐ and ☐ .

13.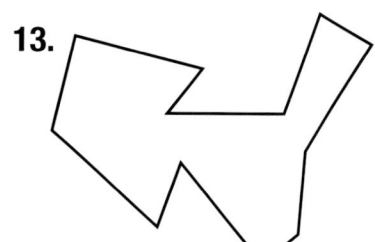
    Use any method you like to find the number of right angles inside this shape.
    _____ right angles.

14. If you use your ruler to measure paths you will find that points (intersections) _____ and _____ in this network are 3.5 cm apart.
    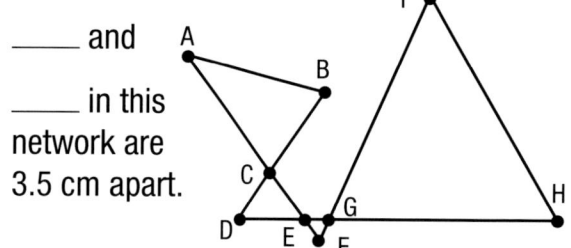

15. How many 10-cm pieces of cotton can be cut from a piece 1½ metres long?
    _____ pieces.

16. Circle each number which is a multiple of both 5 and 10.
    35, 48, 150, 72, 80, 115

17. Shade in the irregular polygon from the shapes below:
    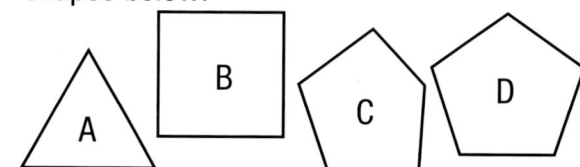

18. Diagram 'A' has 3 inside regions and 8 intersections.
    Diagram 'B' has ☐ inside regions and ☐ intersections.
    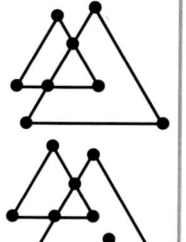

19. 16 x 3 < 4 x 12. True or false?

20. A shape with opposite sides equal and parallel and containing no right angles is a:
    (a) rectangle   (b) square
    (c) trapezium   (d) parallelogram

Set 22 – Revision

1. ¹⁄₁₀ x 2 ≠ ¹⁄₁₀ + ¹⁄₁₀   True or false?

2. Prime Number ☐ + Prime Number ☐ = Composite Number ☐

3. 25% + 0.25 + ⁵⁄₁₀ = _____

4. This prism (a polyhedron) is:
   (a) hexagonal   (b) triangular
   (c) cuboid   (d) pentagonal

5.  In the box rule 3 line segments each 2 cm long and intersecting at 3 points.

6. Complete the letter/number series:
   AA3, AB6, AC9, AD12, _____

7. The angle between the hands of a clock at 2100 hours is:
   (a) 45°   (b) 100°
   (c) 20°   (d) 90°

8. 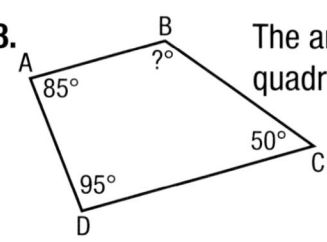 The angles of any quadrilateral (a four-sided shape) total 360° when added.
   Angle ABC = _____°.

9. The fraction ¹⁄₁₀ means:
   (a) one x ten
   (b) one part out of ten parts
   (c) one part out of ten equal parts
   (d) 1 part + 10 parts

10. 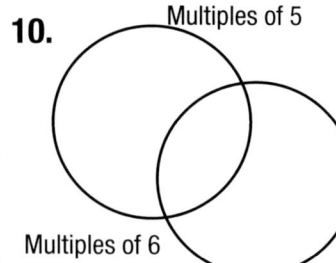 Put the numbers 10, 12, 18, 24, 25, 30 into the Venn diagram. You will have one number in the intersecting set.

11. Write in the boxes the numbers < 40 which have both 2 and 5 as factors.
    ☐ ☐ ☐

12.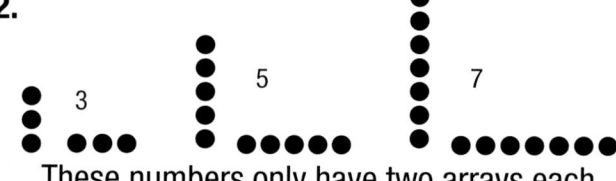
    These numbers only have two arrays each because they are _____ numbers.

13. Find the total length of the vertical line segments (ruler needed).
    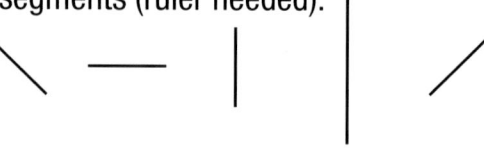
    Total length = _____ mm

14. Circle the 'net' (a polyhedron's flat pattern) for a triangular pyramid.
     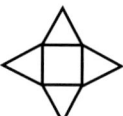 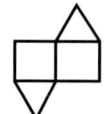 

15. I am a 3-digit number. My last digit is double my middle digit and 4 x my 1st digit which is a prime number. My number is:
    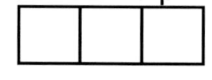

16. How many minutes from 1630 hours to 5.15 p.m.? _____ minutes.

17. Write forty thousand and eleven in figures. _____

18. Shapes 'A' and 'B' are similar shapes.

    True or false?

19. Colour in the right-angled triangle below.
    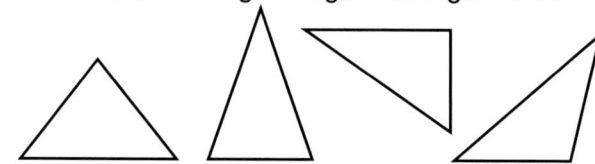

20. Rule a triangle inside the circle so the base of the triangle is a radius of the circle.

Set 23 – Revision

1. ☐ < ⁵⁄₁₀ + ⁴⁄₈

2. Draw a shape which has 4 inside regions in the box.

3. Use the number patterns to complete the last lines:

   3 × 7 = 15 + 5 + 1
   3 × 8 = 15 + 7 + 2
   3 × 9 = 15 + 9 + 3
   3 × 10 = 15 + 11 + 4
   ☐ × ☐ = ☐ + ☐ + ☐

4. Which triangle has only one line (axis) of symmetry?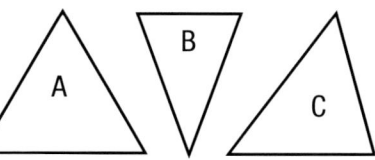

5. Circle the two multiples of 4:
   7, 10, 12, 18, 20, 25

6. Use place value and circle the decimal fraction which is ten times bigger than ⁵⁄₁₀₀
   (a) 0.05   (b) 0.5   (c) 0.005   (d) 0.51

7. Draw 2 triangles which intersect at four points in the box.

8. 3 2 4 7 6
   Put in the decimal point in the number above so that the 7 has a total value of ⁷⁄₁₀.

9. Shade in the right-hand box to make the shaded fractions equivalent fractions.
   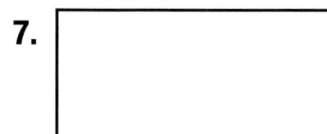 is equivalent to

10. The lengths of the diagonals in rectangles ___ and ___ are the same (ruler needed).
    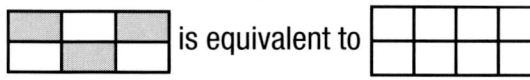

11. A bus route would be measured in:
    (a) mm   (b) cm   (c) m   (d) km

12. Circle the digital clock which shows a time in the afternoon:

13. Write 3 consecutive composite numbers between 10 and 20 in the boxes.
    ☐ ☐ ☐

14. If this shape was rotated clockwise through 180° (90° + 90°) draw the new shape on the cross.
    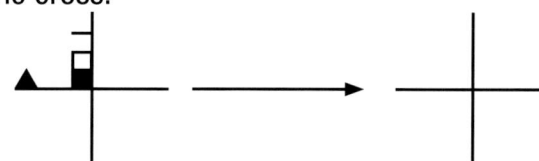

15. ≠ < > =
    Use one of these symbols to make the maths sentence true:
    3 × ¼ ☐ ¼ + ¼ + ¼

16. The perimeter of this square is 40 mm. Its area = _____ mm².

17. I have 5 marbles. Bob has 3 times as many, and David has twice as many as Bob.
    The total number of marbles = _____.

18. The number shown on the abacus is _____.

19. How many of these polygons are irregular shapes (ruler needed)? _____

20. Colour in the 2 shapes which have only one line (axis) of symmetry.
    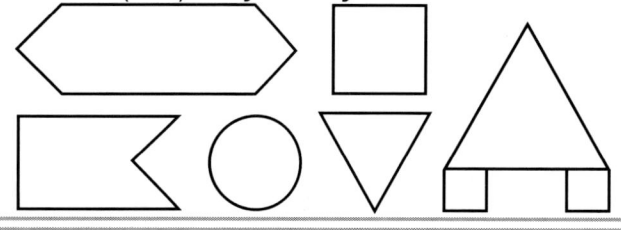

Set 24 – Revision

1. $5 \times \square = 1$

2. The perimeter of this irregular hexagon is < 7 cm. True or false?

3. Circle the numbers which lie between XV and LV.

    LX, XIV, XLV, XXV, LIV

4. $3.047 + 0.03 = $ _____

5. Rule the diagonals in this trapezium and measure their total length.

    _____ mm

6. Which number between 20 and 30 is 4 × the sum of its two digits? _____

7. If I cut along the diagonal of this rectangle what would be the total perimeter of the 2 triangles in millimetres (ruler needed)?

    _____ mm.

8. $0.56 - 0.2 = $ _____

9. You would measure the area of a book's cover in:
    (a) mm²   (b) cm²   (c) m²   (d) km²

10. Follow the patterns and complete the last line:
    20 + 10 = 15 + 15
    30 + 20 = 25 + 25
    40 + 30 = 35 + 35
    50 + 40 = 45 + 45
    ☐ + ☐ = ☐ + ☐

11. What is the sum of the first 5 composite numbers?

    | 1 | 2 | 3 | 4 | 5 | 6 | 7 | 8 | 9 | 10 | 11 | 12 |

12. The length of each side of the small cross has been doubled and this means the area of the large cross is:
    (a) doubled
    (b) 3 × bigger
    (c) 4 × bigger
    (d) 6 × bigger

13. Put in the dimensions (length and width) of this rectangle.

    _____ metres
    Perimeter = 22 m
    Area = 30 m²
    _____ metres

14. The area of the shaded face of this cube is 25 cm². What is the area of the whole surface of the cube?

    _____ cm²

15. There are _____ lengths of wood 20 cm long in a 2-metre plank.

16. 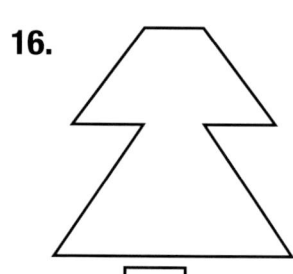 Draw in any lines (axes) of symmetry in this irregular octagon.

17. $4 \times \square = 1.2$

18. Colour in the 2 similar shapes below:

    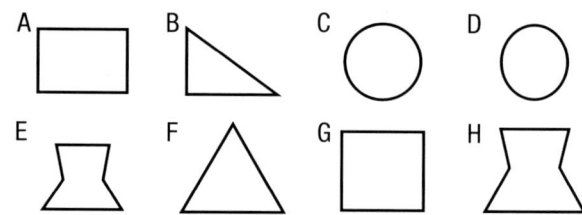

19. How many 25-pence pencils could I buy for £1.50?

    _____ pencils.

20. Rule a vertical diameter in the circle below.

Glossary of terms

acute: describes an angle between 0° and 90°.

adjacent: adjoining (as used to describe lines and angles which are next to each other).

adjacent primes: prime numbers separated by a composite number (e.g. 3, 4, 5).

alternate: every other one in a sequence.

angle: the number of degrees rotated around a point.

anti-clockwise: moving in the opposite direction to the hands on a clock.

arc: part of the circumference of a circle.

area: the amount of space within a perimeter (expressed in square units).

arithmetic mean: the average of a set of numbers.

array: the arrangement of the units of a number in rows and columns (e.g. 6 = : : :).

ascending order: from smallest to largest.

average (mean): a number representing a set of numbers (obtained by dividing the total of the numbers by the number of numbers in the set).

axis (of symmetry): a line dividing a shape into two symmetrical parts.

bar graph: a diagram representing information by the length of bars.

base: the line or face on which a shape is standing.

base angles: those angles adjacent to the base of a shape.

block graph: a diagram representing information by the length of blocks.

capacity: the amount of space in the interior of an object (the amount of liquid/air an object contains).

Carroll diagram: a problem-solving diagram used in classification activities.

chord: a straight line connecting two points on the circumference of a circle.

chronological: describes dates arranged in the order in which they occur (e.g. 1920, 1936, 1992, etc.).

circumference: the distance around a circle (its perimeter).

clockwise: moving in the same direction as the hands of a clock.

closed curve: a curve which has no end points.

common factor: a factor of each of two or more given numbers.

common multiple: a multiple of two or more given numbers.

composite number: a number with more than two factors.

concentric circles: circles which have the same centre point.

congruent: congruent shapes are the same shape and size (equal).

consecutive: consecutive numbers follow in order.

coordinates: numbers used to locate a point on a grid.

cubed: a cubed number is the answer when the square of a number is multiplied by the number itself.

cuboid: a rectangular prism.

cylinder: a circular prism with two congruent, parallel circular end-faces.

denominator: the number below the line in a fraction.

descending order: from largest to smallest.

diagonal: a straight line connecting vertices (corners) of a polygon.

diameter: a straight line connecting two points on the circumference of a circle and passing through the circle's centre.

difference: by how much a number is bigger or smaller than another.

digit: any number from 0 to 9 (inclusive).

digital clock: a clock that shows the time by using numbers rather than hands.

dimensions: the measurements of a shape (i.e. length, width, height).

doubling: multiplying a number or shape by two.

edge: where 2 faces of a 3-D object meet.

equation: a statement of equality between two expressions (e.g. 3 x 4 = 6 + 6).

equilateral triangle: a triangle with congruent (equal) sides and angles.

equivalent: having the same value.

even number: a positive (8) or negative (−6) number exactly divisible by two.

expanded term: written out fully e.g. 2^3 = 2 x 2 x 2

face: a plane surface of a three-dimensional object.

face value: the numeral itself despite its position in a number (e.g. face value of the 5 in 3520 is 5).

factor: a number which will divide exactly into another number.

factorial: the product of all the numbers from 1 to a given number (e.g. the factorial of 4 is 1 x 2 x 3 x 4 = 24).

Fibonacci numbers: a series of numbers in which any number is the sum of the previous two.

fraction: an amount expressed in terms of a numerator and a denominator (usually part of a whole).

heptagon: a plane shape with seven sides and seven angles.

Glossary of terms

hexagon: a polygon with six sides and six angles.

hexagonal: having the shape of a hexagon.

hexahedron: a three-dimensional shape with six faces.

horizontal: a line parallel to the Earth's surface.

improper fraction: a fraction whose numerator is equal to or greater than its denominator.

index notation: a short way of writing the repeated multiplication of numbers. e.g 4^3

integer: a negative or positive whole number (e.g. … –2, –1, 0, 1, 2 …).

interior angles: the angles inside a shape.

intersection: the point where two lines cross or two faces meet.

irregular shapes: shapes which do not have all congruent sides and all congruent angles.

isosceles triangle: a triangle with two congruent sides and two congruent angles.

line graph: a diagram using straight lines to join points representing certain information.

line segment: a line with two end points.

mapping diagram: a diagram showing the relationship between sets of information by using arrows.

mass: the amount of matter in an object (its weight on Earth).

mean (arithmetic mean): the average of a set of numbers, (see average).

median: in statistics, the middle measurement when information is arranged in order of size (e.g. 5 is the median of 2, 3, 5, 10, 13). Where there is no middle score, an average of the two central scores is taken.

mixed number: a symbol representing a whole number and a fraction (e.g. $2\frac{3}{8}$).

modal score (mode): in statistics, the measurement that occurs most often. (e.g. the modal score of 2, 7, 4, 4, 3, 4, 9, 4 is 4).

multiples: the multiples of a number are those numbers which a given number will divide into exactly (e.g. some multiples of 3 are 3, 12, 21, 60, etc.).

net: a flat pattern that can be folded to make a three-dimensional model of a shape.

network: a system of lines (paths) and nodes (points representing intersections).

numeral: a symbol used to represent a number (e.g. 5 and V are numerals representing the number 5).

numerator: the number above the line in a fraction.

obtuse angle: an angle between 90° and 180°.

octagon: a polygon with eight sides and eight angles.

octahedron: a polyhedron (three-dimensional shape) with eight faces.

odd number: a number that when divided by two leaves a remainder of one.

parallel lines: lines always the same distance apart.

parallelogram: a four-sided polygon with opposite sides equal and parallel and containing no right angles.

path: a line connecting nodes (points) in a network.

pentagon: a polygon with five sides and five angles.

pentomino: a plane shape made of five congruent squares connected to each other by at least one common side.

percentage: a quantity expressed in hundredths.

perfect number: a number which is the sum of its factors apart from itself (e.g. 6 = 1 + 2 + 3).

perimeter: the length of the distance around the boundary of a shape.

perpendicular line: a line at right angles to another line or plane.

pie graph: a circular graph in which sectors of a circle are used to show information.

place value: indicates the position of a numeral (e.g. the place value of the 3 in the number 357 is hundreds).

plane shape: level, flat, two-dimensional.

polygon: a two-dimensional shape with three or more straight lines.

polyhedron (plural – polyhedra): a three-dimensional shape with plane faces.

prime factor: a prime number that will divide exactly into another number (e.g. 2 and 3 are prime factors of 6).

prime number: a number with only two factors, 1 and itself.

prism: a three-dimensional shape with at least one pair of opposite faces which are congruent and parallel.

product: the result when two or more numbers are multiplied (e.g. the product of 2, 3, 4 is 2 x 3 x 4 = 24).

proper fraction (vulgar fraction): a fraction in which the numerator is less than the denominator.

property: an attribute of a two-dimensional or three-dimensional shape.

protractor: a semi-circular or circular instrument for measuring angles.

pyramid: a square base and four triangular sides meeting at a common vertex.

quadrant: a quarter of the area of a circle which also contains a right angle.

quadrilateral: any four-sided polygon.

radius: a line joining the centre of a circle to a point on the circle's circumference.

Glossary of terms

rectangle: a quadrilateral with opposite sides equal and parallel and containing four right angles (a square is a rectangle).

reflex angle: an angle greater than 180°.

region: the interior area enclosed by a perimeter (the area outside the perimeter is the exterior region).

regular shape: a polygon is regular if all its sides and angles are congruent (opposite – irregular).

rhombus: a parallelogram with congruent sides and containing no right angles (a diamond shape).

right angle: an angle containing 90°.

right-angled triangle: a triangle containing one right angle (90°).

rotating: turning in a clockwise or anti-clockwise direction.

scalene triangle: a triangle with sides of different length and three different interior angles.

sector: the part of a circle bounded by two radii and the included arc.

segment: the part of a circle bounded by a chord and an arc.

semi-circle: half a circle (the area bounded by a diameter and an arc).

similar shapes: have the same shape but differ in size.

simplify: to change to simpler terms (e.g. $^{45}/_{60}$ to $^{3}/_{4}$)

solid shape: a three-dimensional shape (with length, width, height).

sphere: a completely round three-dimensional shape.

squared: a number squared is multiplied by itself.

square number: a number whose units can be arranged into a square (e.g. 4 : :).

sum: the result when two or more numbers are added.

supplementary angles: two angles which, when added, total 180° (as in a straight line).

surface area: the total area of all the faces of a three-dimensional shape.

symmetrical: a shape is symmetrical if it is identical on either side of a line dividing it into two parts. A mirror image.

tally: a record of items using vertical and oblique lines to represent each item.

tessellating shapes: shapes which will cover an area leaving no gaps between them.

tetrahedron: a polyhedron with four faces (e.g. triangular pyramid).

tetromino: a plane shape made of four congruent squares connected to each other by at least one common side.

three (3-)dimensional shape: a shape with length, width and height.

total: the result when two or more numbers are added.

total place value: what total quantity a numeral represents according to its position in a number.

trapezium: a quadrilateral with two parallel sides.

traversable: a network is traversable if it can be traced over without going over the same path twice.

triangular number: a number whose units can be arranged into a triangle (e.g. 6).

tromino: a plane shape made of three congruent squares connected to each other by at least one common side.

Venn diagram: a diagram which shows sets and their relationships.

vertex (plural – vertices): the point at which two or more lines or edges meet.

vertical line: a line which is at right angles to a horizontal line.

volume: the amount of space taken up by an object.

Symbols Used

>	greater than
=	is equal to
≈	is approximately equal to
<	less than
≠	is not equal to

Pupil assessment

Class:												Record sheet					of							
Pupil Name	\multicolumn{24}{c}{**Work Sets 1–24**}
	1	2	3	4	5	6	7	8	9	10	11	12	13	14	15	16	17	18	19	20	21	22	23	24

Pupil assessment

Class:												Record sheet					of							
Pupil Name	Revision Sets 1–24																							
	1	2	3	4	5	6	7	8	9	10	11	12	13	14	15	16	17	18	19	20	21	22	23	24

Answers

Set 1
1. 63
2. 5321
3. (b)
4. ■□□□□
5. 36 ÷ 9 = 4
6. 5012
7. 8
8. 48
9. 07:00
10. ▼□▲▲
11. (a)
12. 7 cm
13. 3 x 8 = 18 + 6
14. 3 regions
15.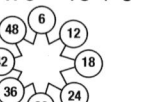

Set 2
1. 20
2. answer varies
3. 40
4. 15p
5. 6
6. (d)
7. (c)
8. V
9. (c)
10. 11
11. 3, Roy
12. •, ••••, or ••
13. 15 mm
14. 6 faces, 12 edges
15. ²⁄₄

Set 3
1.
2. (c)
3.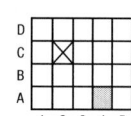
4. 5 x 80 = 400
5. 125cm
6. (diagram)
7. 3 out of 8
8. answer varies
9. 40 mm line, 10 mm segments
10. (c)
11. 427
12. 2 x 6 x 2
13. (grid)
14. (trapezium)
15. 25 mm

Set 4
1. (c)
2. (b)
3. 20, 2
4. £2.00
5. D, A
6. £7.60
7. (square diagram)
8. (b)
9.
10. 20 + 10 + 30
11. 18 edges
12. 864
13. (trapezium)
14. 15°C
15. 20

Set 5
1. (b)
2. 3 x 5 + 9 = 10 + 14
3. 0
4. (dot pattern)
5. 2 cm, 1 cm
6. 8, 26, 12
7. 8.72 m, 7.05 m
8. (d)
9. £8.05
10. ↓↓↓↓→
11. toy
12. Bible
13. 14
14. (grid)
15. (c)

Set 6
1. 4014
2. (c)
3. £10 £5 10p £1 5p £2 20p 50p
4. (diagram)
5. 5
6. 700
7. 25 mm
8. 2346
9. 30 mm
10. 999, 1000, 1001
11. answer varies
12. 16 cm
13. E, B
14. 17, 13
15. 16

Set 7
1. 24000
2. 16 x 5 = 8 x 10
3. 6, 3, 5, 21
4. (b)
5. 16
6. 1½ metres
7. (d) 5-sided
8. 4
9. two
10. (c)
11. rectangles have same perimeter
12. 7 lots
13. the 22nd
14. ○○○○○○○●
15. (diagram)

Set 8
1. XI or 11
2. answers vary
3. odd
4. IJ4, KL2
5. C, D
6. answers vary
7. (a)
8. 7, 37, 359, 1021
9. Tim, May, Amy, Rod
10. 300
11. (c)
12. (grid)
13. 6 inside regions
14. C, D
15. £4.50

Set 9
1. 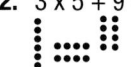, 25
2. 581
3. (clock)
4. 732
5. (c)
6. (c)
7. 20 cm²
8. 1½ cm, 15 mm
9. 9 children
10. 4 times
11. (1 x 12) 2 = 10
12. answers vary
13. 32
14. Tim, Roy
15. 16 cm

Answers

Set 10
1. < (less than)
2. 5
3. E
4. even
5. answers vary
6. broom, bed
7.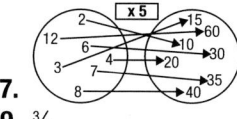
8. (d)
9. ⅜
10. 12 x 9 - 8 = 100
11.
12. Peter, David, Amy, June
13. £1
14.
15. 1 cm, 10 mm

Set 11
1. (d)
2. either top or bottom
3. =
4. 16.00
5. ⅒, ¼, ½
6. (b)
7. (b)
8.
9.
10. 44 cubes
11. Mary £12, John £4, Rhonda, £6
12. 20 mm segments
13.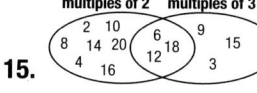
14. 24
15.

Set 12
1. 8 + 8 + 8
2. 3000+300+30+3
3. (c)
4. 4
5.
6. (c)
7. (d)
8. £88
9. odd, even
10. (d)
11. 17 fifties
12. inside, outside
13. 9
14. 13 cm, 130 mm
15.

Set 13
1. = (equals)
2. 30
3. 2.11
4. 3 5 7 11 13 17 19
5. 500 metres
6. ²⁄₁₀
7. 1
8.
9. 2 600
10. 30
11.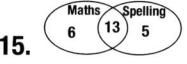
12.
13. 13:00 or .01.00
14. (c)
15. 5 x 3000 = 10000 + 5000
16. 4 cm or 40 mm
17. B is double A
18. (c)
19. true
20. 70 km/hr

Set 14
1. seven thousand, two hundred and eight
2. 6 m
3. False
4. 10
5. 21 cubes
6. 1200 ml
7. C is longer than B
8. 15000 ÷ 5 = 3000
9. 20 x 40
10. ⅛
11. 31502
12.
13.
14. 24 pupils
15. 3 x (4 + 1) = 15
16. 20 liked chocolate, 12 liked both, 5 liked only cake
17. C, E
18.
19. yes
20.

Set 15
1. 20
2.
3.
4. XXI
5. 2 cm
6. (c)
7.
8. 50-37=13
9. (4 + 6) + 2 = 4 + (6 + 2)
10. 9, 15
11. 27 cubes
12. (c)
13. 2 x 2 x 2 x 2 x 2
14. 5 regions
15.
16.
17. (d)
18. answer on sheet
19.
20. 12 or 13 cm

Set 16
1. (c)
2. 23458
3. 4207
4. (a)
5. false
6.
7.
8. (c)
9. (a)
10.
11. 223, 241, 221
12.
13.
14. 1 x 2 x 3, 1 + 2 + 3
15. 30 ÷ 6 = 5, 5 x 6 = 30, 6 x 5 = 30
16. D and E
17. £55
18.
19. yes
20.

Answers

Set 17
1. 485
2. true
3. $^{10}/_{10}$,
4. GH3, IJ1
5. A and C
6.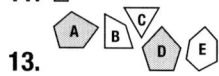
7. 427, 472, 724, 742
8. (a)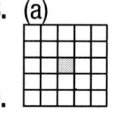
9. (c)
10.
11.
12.
13.
14. 3
15. (b)
16. 2 x 3 x 5
17. false
18.
19.
20. 1500 metres

Set 18
1. (c)
2. $^3/_{10} + ^5/_{100}$
3. (a)
4. 30
5. (D)
6. (7 x 1000) – 7 = 6993
7. (c)
8.
9.
10.
11. £12
12. 1½ cm or 15 mm
13. 130 cm
14. V
15. 60 km
16.
17.
18.
19. (d)
20. 7 cm²

Set 19
1. 0
2. 1952, 1908, 1992
3.
4. 14 cm or 140 mm
5. 0.2, 2.0, 2.02, 2.2, 2.22
6. ⁴⁄₈, ³⁄₆
7.
8.
9. (c)
10. (c)
11. 999
12.
13. answers vary
14.
15.
16. (c)

Their sum	Their product	Numbers used
13	30	10 and 3
11	28	**7 and 4**
9	20	**5 and 4**

17. (d)
18.
19.
20. 9 3 4 5
    – 2 **8 7 8**
       6 4 **6** 7

Set 20
1. (c)
2. 4
3. (b)
4. 5
5. (c)
6. > (greater than)
7. 1114
8.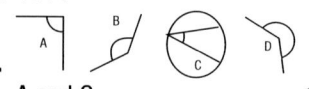
9.
10. A and C
11. (c)
12. 60000 ÷ 3 = 10000 + 10000
13. 4 tenths
14. B, A
15.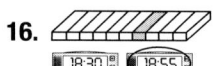
16.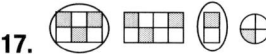
17. (November calendar with 23 circled)
18. 5 cm
19. (c)
20. (c)

Set 21
1. (c)
2. (b)
3. (c)
4. 2
5. (c)
6. (number line 50–275, 200 circled)
7. ○○○○○○○
8. (number pyramid)
9. E, A
10. (d)
11. 12 and 8
12. 5
13. A and H
14. 375 (only odd number)
15. 8 pieces
16. 1203, 1312
17.
18. 7 inside regions and 6 intersections
19. false
20. (c)

Set 22
1. false
2. answers vary
3. 1½
4. (c)
5. answers vary
6. I4
7. , (b)
8. 100°
9. (d)
10. (Venn diagram: multiples of 3 {9, 6}, shared {12}, multiples of 4 {8, 16, 20})
11.
12. 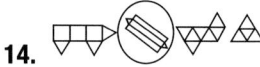, 3½ cm
13. prime numbers
14.
15.
16. 25 minutes
17. true
18. 13 006
19.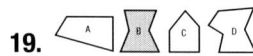
20. answers vary

#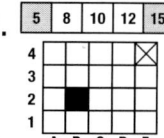

Set 23
1. answers vary (less than one)
2. answers vary
3. 3 x 11 = 20 + 9 + 4
4. answers vary
5. 12, 15
6. (a)
7. answers vary
8. 23•756
9. shade 2 squares
10. C
11. (b)
12.
13.
14.
15. = (equals)
16. 40 mm
17. 90 marbles
18. (c)
19.
20.

Set 24
1. ¹⁄₁₀ or 0.1
2. false
3. 2.063
4. 1049, 1498
5. 6 cm
6. 36
7. 10 cm
8. 0.18
9. (b)
10. 16 + 4 = 10 + 10, 18 + 4 = 11 + 11
11. , 28
12. Perimeter = 22 m, Area = 24 m²
13. (b)
14. 96 cm²
15. 20 pieces
16. 0.5
17.
18.
19. 7 pencils
20. (answers vary)

Set 1 – Revision
1. 105
2. C
3. 1347
4.
5. 35 ÷ 7 = 5
6. 7002
7. 8
8. 100
9. 19:30
10.
11. (c)
12. 8 cm
13. 5 x 8 = 30 + 10
14. 8
15.

Set 2 – Revision
1. 24
2. answers vary
3. 70
4. 12
5. 8
6. (c)
7. (c)
8. V
9. (b)
10. ⁵⁄₁₀
11. B, F, C
12. 10
13.
14. 8 vertices
15. 25 mm

Set 3 – Revision
1.
2. (d)
3.
4. 10 x 80 = 800
5. 175 cm
6.
7. answers vary
8. 7 out of 10
9. 60 mm line divided into 30 mm lengths
10. (d)
11. 234
12. 2 x 5 x 2
13.
14.
15. 15 mm

Set 4 – Revision
1. (d)
2. (c)
3. 12, 10
4. 36 marbles
5. D is 3x A
6. £58.00
7.
8. (c)
9.
10. 2 + 4 + 8
11. 600
12. 15 edges
13. square divided into 4 2-cm squares
14. 36
15. 100, 40

Set 5 – Revision
1. (c)
2. (5 x 5) + 10 = 24 + 11
3. one number is 0
4.
5. B, C, D
6. 15, 21, 42, 99
7. 6.23 m, 2.07 m
8. (c)
9.
10. HOT
11. £1
12. SOIL
13.
14. 36
15. 19 squares

Set 6 – Revision
1. 5012
2. (b)
3.
4.
5. 4 vertices
6. 2138
7. 500
8. 20 mm
9. 1100, 1101, 1102
10. 50 mm
11. answers vary
12. 17 cm
13. F, E
14. IX, XXI, XII, XVI, VII, XIV, XV
15. 14 cubes

Answers

Set 7 – Revision
1. 37000
2. 22 x 6 = 11 x 12
3. 2½, 1½, 3½
4. (b)
5. 19
6. 2.5 or 2½
7. D
8. 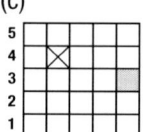 (6)
9. eight
10. (e)
11.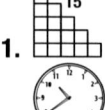
12. B and A
13. 9
14. 250 lots
15. ◐○⊕⊕○○⊖ (answers vary)

Set 8 – Revision
1. XXX
2. answers vary
3. even
4. AE12, AF14
5. (3D shapes)
6. answers vary
7. 8, 2768, 3020, 1084
8. (b)
9. Bob, Ann, Ian, Roy
10. 500
11. (c)
12. (grid: 24 28 20 / 30 36 16 / 40 12 60)
13. 5
14. A, E, C, F
15. Amy £12, Ann £3, Toni £5

Set 9 – Revision
1.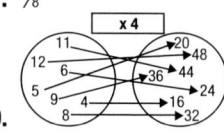
2. 742, smallest no. = 247
3. (clock)
4. 574
5. (c)
6. (d)
7. 18 cm²
8. 2½ cm, 25 mm
9. John 8, Sue 16
10. (6 x 8) = 36 + 12
11. 4 + 1 = 2 + 3
12. 4 times
13. 21
14. 19 cm
15. Rose, Paul

Set 10 – Revision
1. > (greater than)
2. 10
3. C
4. odd
5. answers vary
6. door, brick, car
7. ⅝
8. (d)
9.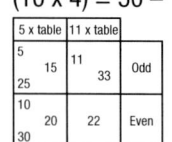
10. £2
11. (10 x 4) = 50 – 10
12.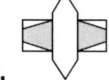
13. (table: 5x table / 11x table / 5, 11, Odd / 15, 33 / 25 / 10, 22, Even / 30, 20)
15. Mary, Pat, Jean, Alan

Set 11 – Revision
1. (c)
2.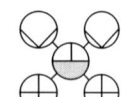
3. = (equals)
4. 13:00
5. ¹⁄₂₀, ¼, ½
6. (d)
7. (c)
8. C
9.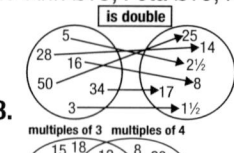
10. 42 cubes
11. Ann £15, Peta £10, Roy £5
12. (triangle diagram)
13. (is double diagram: 5→2½, 28→14, 16→8, 50→25, 34→17, 3→1½)
14. 30
15. (Venn: multiples of 3 {15,18,6,9,21}, both {12,24}, multiples of 4 {20,8,16})

Set 12 – Revision
1. 4
2. 4
3. (c)
4. 5000+500+50+5
5. (shapes)
6. (b)
7. (c)
8. £35
9. 14 fifties
10. 7 cm or 70 mm
11. (a)
12. outside, inside
13. 9
14. odd, even
15. (Venn: Sport 8, both 14, Art 9)

Set 13 – Revision
1. = (equals)
2. 72
3. 1.13
4. (9 15 21 25 27)
5. 1200 m
6. ⁵⁄₁₂
7. 2 x 5 x 11
8. (3D shapes)
9. 3630
10. 40
11. ||||·||||·||||·|||
12. (angles)
13. 15:30
14. 4 x 10 = 25 + 15
15. (d)
16. 1½ cm or 15 mm
17. (b)
18. C, A
19. false
20. Monday, Tuesday

Set 14 – Revision
1. four thousand and six
2. 3 m
3. false
4. 3
5. 22
6. 170 kg
7. C, A
8. 24000 ÷ 3 = 4000 + 4000
9. 50 x 20
10. ⁵⁄₁₀
11. 30152
12. 1
13. (triangles)
14. (circle with arrow)
15. 24
16. 27 liked summer, 4 liked both, 2 liked only winter
17. Sam, May
18. (rectangle) (3)
19. no
20. rubber, rock, coin, sock, fruit

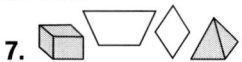 Answers

Set 15 – Revision

1. 30
2.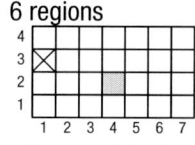
3. (dice image)
4. VIII
5. 3 cm
6. (b)
7. (shapes)
8. 8
9. 4
10. 27 33 35 39
11. 64 cubes
12. (b)
13. 1 x 1 x 1 x 1 = 1
14. 6 regions
15. (shape)
16. (grid)
17. (c)
18. (shapes)
19. answer on sheet
20. 15 or 16 cm

Set 16 – Revision

1. (d)
2. 23 479
3. 207.3
4. $^3/_8$
5. false
6. (table)
7.
8. (d)
9. (c)
10. (shapes)
11. 1100, 1099
12. (dots)
13. (trapezium)
14. ½
15. 40 ÷ 5 = 8, 5 x 8 = 40, 8 x 5 = 40
16. A and H
17. £35
18.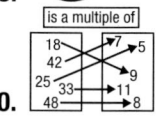
19. yes
20. (diagram)

Set 17 – Revision

1. 983
2. true
3. $^8/_8$, $^5/_5$
4. QR12, ST15
5. A and G
6. 42 44 45 46 48 49
7. 326, 623, 362, 632
8. (b)
9. (c)
10. (grid)
11.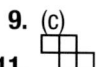
12. (fractions)
13. answers vary
14. 10
15. (b)
16. 2 x 5 x 7
17. true
18. (shapes)
19. 750 g
20. (dots)

Set 18 – Revision

1. (b)
2. $^6/_{10} + ^3/_{100}$
3. (c)
4. 20
5.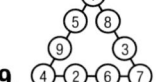
6. (5 x 1000) – 5 = 4995
7. (b)
8. (shape)
9.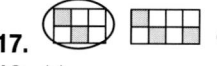
10. (shapes A B C D)
11. £7
12. 8½ cm
13. 140 cm
14. VI
15. 75 km
16. (shape)
17.
18. (clocks)
19. (c)
20. 4 cm²

Set 19 – Revision

1. 0
2. 1964, 1972
3. 15 21 27 33 39
4. 56 cm or 560 mm
5. 2.8, 2.51, 2.08, 2.02, 0.88
6. $^1/_3$, $^2/_6$
7. (lines)
8. (clocks)
9. (b)
10. (c)
11. 998
12. (shape)
13. answers vary
14. (shape)
15.
16. 37 years
17. D

Their sum	Their product	Numbers used
15	50	10 and 5
11	24	**3** and **8**
7	12	3 and 4

19. (shapes A B C D)
20.

Set 20 – Revision

1. (b)
2. 3 lengths
3. (c)
4. 92 days
5. (c)
6. > (greater than)
7. 1215
8.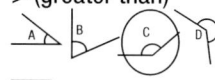
9. 7 x 6 = 42 = 40 + 2
10. (shape)
11. (c)
12. (b) and (c)
13. (shape), 2
14. A and C
15. (dots) ...
16. 2
17. (March calendar, 25 circled)
18. 7 cm
19. (c)
20. (b)

Prim-Ed Publishing—www.prim-ed.com   Mental Mathematics Practice Book 1   59

Answers

Set 21 – Revision
1. (c)
2. (c)
3. (c)
4. 24
5. (c)
6. 0.3 0.6 0.9 ... 2.1
7. ○○○○○○○○
8. (pyramid of numbers: 3 / 3 6 3 / 3 6 9 6 3 / 3 6 9 12 9 6 3 / 3 6 9 12 15 12 9 6 3)
9. D, G
10. (c)
11. 13 (prime no.)
12. 9 and 7
13. 3,
14. I and F
15. 15 pieces
16. 150, 80
17.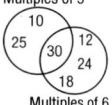
18. 5 inside regions and 13 intersections
19. false
20. (d)

Set 22 – Revision
1. false
2. answers vary
3. 1
4. (d)
5. answers vary
6. AE15
7. (clock), (d)
8. 130°
9. (c)
10. (Venn diagram: Multiples of 5 / Multiples of 6, 10, 25, 30, 12, 24, 18)
11. 10 20 30
12. prime
13. 40 mm
14. (shapes)
15. 2 4 8
16. 45 minutes
17. 40 011
18. true
19. (triangles)
20. (circle with angle) (answers vary)

Set 23 – Revision
1. answers vary (less than one)
2. answers vary
3. 3 × 11 = 15 + 13 + 5
4. B
5. 12, 20
6. (b)
7. (answers vary)
8. 324•76
9. (grid)
10. B and D
11. (d)
12. (digital clocks: 07:30, 23:00, 14:30, 11:50)
13. 14 15 16
14. (diagram)
15. = (equals)
16. 100 mm²
17. 50 marbles
18. 210.32
19. 3,
20. (shapes)

Set 24 – Revision
1. ⅕
2. true
3. XLV, XXV, LIV
4. 3.077
5. 50 mm
6. 24
7. 130 mm
8. 0.36
9. (b)
10. 60 + 50 = 55 + 55
11. 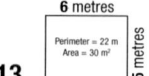, 37
12. (c)
13. 6 metres, 5 metres, Perimeter = 22 m, Area = 30 m²
14. 150 cm²
15. 10 lengths
16. (shape)
17. 0.3
18. (shapes A B C D E F G H)
19. 6 pencils
20. (circle)